The
Complete Book
of
Gourd
Craft

The
Complete Book
of

Gourd
Craft

22 Projects
55 Decorative Techniques
300 Inspirational Designs

Ginger Summit

Jim Widess

Lark Books
Asheville, North Carolina

DEDICATION

In memory of Linda Lindberg, friend and mentor to gourd lovers around the world.

EDITOR: **Deborah Morgenthal**
ART DIRECTOR: **Chris Bryant**
PRODUCTION: **Chris Bryant**
PHOTOGRAPHY: **Jim Widess** (unless otherwise noted)

Library of Congress Cataloging-in-Publication Data

Summit, Ginger.
    The complete book of gourd craft: 22 projects, 55 decorative techniques,
    300 inspirational designs / Ginger Summit and Jim Widess
        p.   cm.
    Includes bibliographical references and index.
    ISBN 0-937274-99-2
    1. Gourd craft.   I. Widess, Jim.   II. Title
    TT873.5.S86   1996
    745.5—dc20   95-46760
                                            CIP

10 9 8 7 6 5 4 3 2

Published in 1996 by Lark Books
50 College Street
Asheville, NC 28801

© 1996 by Ginger Summit and Jim Widess

Distributed in the U.S. by Sterling Publishing
    387 Park Avenue South, New York, NY 10016; 1-800-367-9692

Distributed in Canada by Sterling Publishing,
    c/o Canadian Manda Group, One Atlantic Avenue, Suite 105, Toronto, Ontario, Canada M6K 3E7

Distributed in Great Britain and Europe by Cassell PLC,
    Wellington House, 125 Strand, London, England WC2R OBB

Distributed in Australia by Capricorn Link (Australia) Pty Ltd.,
    P.O. Box 6651, Baulkham Hills Business Centre, NSW, Australia 2153

Printed in Hong Kong.

ISBN 0-937274-99-2

Contents

Introduction

History and Culture

WHERE GOURDS ORIGINATED

The gourd plant has been described as one of nature's greatest gifts to mankind. Of all the known plants, the gourd is the only one experts believe spanned the entire globe in prehistoric times. It appears as one of the first cultivated plants in regions throughout the world and was used by every known culture in the Temperate and Tropical Zones.

Even with this background, it is surprising how little is actually known of the origins of the gourd family. And, although tantalizing hints of the gourd's historic usefulness do exist, the physical evidence is frustratingly limited, fragmented, and scattered. Gourds don't last long when they aren't specifically cared for; the few gourd artifacts that have been discovered and preserved are widely separated, not only by continents and oceans, but by thousands of years.

The very earliest gourd specimens are seeds and fragments that were unearthed in Ayacucho, Peru, dating from 10,000 B.C., from the Ocampo Caves in Mexico, dating from 10,000 to 7,000 B.C., and just recently from Gainesville, Florida, dating from 11,000 B.C. The oldest evidence of a gourd in North America are seeds found along with the remains of a mastodon. Other archaeological explorations throughout Florida have found numerous gourd seeds, fragments—and in one case—an intact gourd, all associated with early human settlements, dating from as early as 6,000 B.C. Additional evidence suggests that gourds were probably one of the first cultivated plants in the mid-Mississippi region between 3,000 to 2,000 B.C.

Recent investigations have identified several varieties of small wild gourds that are believed to be native to North America: *c. okeechobenis* from Florida, *c. texana* from the Mississippi Valley area, the ozarkana from eastern North America, and the buffalo gourd from the more arid regions of the Southwest.

With so much physical evidence tying the gourd to the Western Hemisphere, it could be assumed that the gourd plant originated in this area. However, botanists have identified many wild ancestors of the gourd plant in Africa, a fact that indicates that the hardshell *lagenaria* gourd plant first originated in Africa. Research conducted in California in 1954 suggests that gourds drifted in oceanic currents to various landfalls in the Western Hemisphere, including locations throughout the east coast of what is now South America, the Middle Americas, and Florida. Gourds probably were growing in this hemisphere long before humans began to arrive around 12,000 B.C. An excellent review of this issue can be found in *The Gourd Book*, by Charles Heiser.

Peru, dating circa 100 B.C. (Nasca-II phase). Carved decorations depict mystical beings holding human victims.

PHOEBE HEARST MUSEUM, BERKELEY, CALIFORNIA

Butter container from the Songhrai of Mali. Lower portion of goatskin covering is the udder of the goat, with the teats forming the legs to balance the gourd.

COLLECTION OF AMI DIALLO   PHOTO BY SUE SMITH

Milk container, from Samburo of Kenya, Africa.
Protected by leather straps decorated with glass beads.

COLLECTION OF JUDY MULFORD

PHOTO BY JUDY MULFORD

THE ROLE OF GOURDS IN WORLD CULTURES

By examining the gourds that have been preserved in museums and collections around the world, by analyzing folk tales and religious mythology from diverse cultures, and by studying the uses of gourds in contemporary cultures, we are able to deduce some of the rich contributions that gourds have made in the social and cultural evolution of humankind.

Gourds played an important role in the changes that took place as humans became tool users and masters of their environment. Evidence from Florida and the Ocampo Caves in Mexico indicates that gourds were used as containers long before baskets or pottery served that purpose. Samples of the oldest known pottery imitate the familiar shapes of bottle gourds, suggesting that the bottle gourd was familiar to, and most likely used by, the earliest cultures not only in Africa and North America, but in Asia, too. Primitive basketry techniques in the form of vine webbing and cordage have been found wrapped around ancient gourds in both Peru and Florida: the webbing served as handles and protective covering, and to attach gourd floats to nets for fishing.

As horticultural practices began to develop, certain gourd seeds may have been deliberately planted to ensure the reproduction of the most useful gourd varieties and shapes. Every part of the plant was used. In many cultures, the fruits were probably eaten while they were still quite small, as they are today in many parts of the world. When the fruit was mature, the seeds were undoubtedly used for food as well, as they are very high in protein and oils. Most primitive cultures found medicinal uses for the gourd root, leaf, stem, flower, and fruit.

Mate, a tea made from the leaves of a small bush that is grown in Argentina and Chile, is traditionally drunk only from gourd cups, using straws made of metal to strain the tea.

PHOEBE HEARST MUSEUM, BERKELEY, CALIFORNIA

By far the most common uses of gourds in all cultures were as containers and vessels. They were used to store every manner of supplies, wet and dry, food and utility, domestic and otherwise. Hauling and storage of water was of paramount concern in every tribe regardless of locale. Gourd dippers, ladles, and containers representing all periods of civilization are seen in museums throughout Africa, Asia, the Western Hemisphere, and the Pacific Islands. In Africa and North America, all manner of foods were stored in gourds, even when other vessels were available. In New Zealand, bird and rat meat was preserved in its own fat and stored in decorated gourds for special occasions. Salt and honey were collected, transported, traded or sold, and then stored in their own gourd containers. American settlers felt that eggs lasted longer and were safer from pests if they were kept in a special bushel gourd.

In addition to storing and transporting foods, gourds were also used as cooking and eating utensils. Native Americans boiled food by dropping hot rocks into gourds filled with liquids. Many gourd ladles from Middle America and the Southwest are scorched on the bottom, evidence of their use to pour and spread batter on the cooking stones. Gourd sake bottles in Japan are family heirlooms, whose care is traditionally entrusted to the eldest son. In Africa and the Americas, babies were fed from bottles made of small hardshell gourds, and many were bathed and even rocked to sleep in large gourds.

Gourds were and still are used to make and ferment drinks. The Masai in Kenya, Africa, collected blood in gourds from an incision made in the jugular vein of cows, which was then mixed with milk and honey or urine. This mixture was allowed to ferment for several days, until it was drunk by the men preparing to go on a hunt or warring party. Beer made from various grains or plants was mixed and fermented in gourds throughout the Americas. In Hawaii, poi was mixed in huge gourds and allowed to ferment for several weeks. It was also served from other special gourd platters. In all of these situations, the gourd itself was thought to have special properties that made it uniquely suitable for the fermenting process.

The balaphon consists of gourds that are suspended under wooden slats and is played much like a marimba.

COLLECTION OF PETER BOHLEY

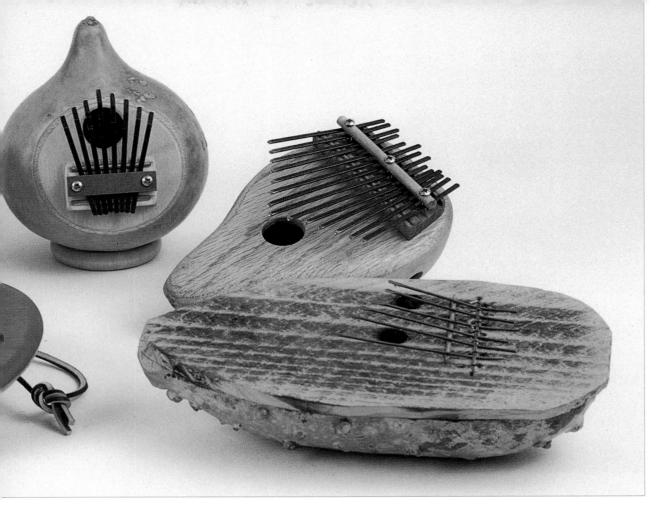

Men and women on several continents chewed betel nut mixed with crushed lime, which was carried in special gourd containers. Rubbing oils and body dyes, medicine, seeds, bait, and gunpowder were stored and carried in specially constructed gourd canteens.

Gourd musical instruments have been identified in every recorded ancient culture, and the forms they take are remarkably diverse. The type most frequently found is the rattle, in which additional seeds, pebbles, or shells either are added to the inside or are included in the lacing around the outside of the gourd. The gourd was frequently used as a resonator; drums and balaphons (marimbalike instruments in which gourds are suspended beneath wooden strips connected on a long frame) represent the wide range of forms these assumed. Gourds were also used as horns, whistles, and flutes, assuming fantastic shapes and purposes, from lovers' whistles in Hawaii to cobra enchanters in India. Stringed instruments ranged from the single-stringed berimbau to the multiple-stringed gourd harp, including the familiar gourd banjo and fiddle. The most elaborate stringed instruments were perfected in India in the form of the vina and sitar. Another familiar gourd instrument is the thumb piano, or mbira, which has several names and variations, depending on use and culture. Most of these instruments, while ancient in origin, are still being used today in many forms throughout the world.

The Huichol Indians of Mexico created elaborate and brilliant designs of sacred symbols on the inside of gourd bowls, using small beads pressed into warm beeswax.
COLLECTION OF GINGER SUMMIT

Gourds were also used as birdhouses and feeders. European explorers noted gourd birdhouses in native villages in North America. In China, gourds were not used as houses for the birds, but were fashioned into unique bird whistles. These small whistles were fastened to the bodies of pigeons, and as the birds flew overhead, owners could identify their pets by the sounds.

Gourds were used as clothing, too. Hats fashioned of gourds were worn in China, Mexico, South America, and Africa. In New Guinea, men in certain mountain tribes continue to wear gourds as penis sheaths. The specific rationale behind this unusual piece of clothing is not very well understood.

In Haiti, the gourd became valued not only for its functional uses, but was turned into an actual item of currency. According to numerous accounts, in 1807 when Henri Christophe became governor of Haiti after the abolition of slavery, the country was bankrupt. People were entirely dependent on wild produce, and gourds were useful not only as utensils in daily life but also as a source of food. Chief Christophe declared that every green gourd in the country was the property of the state, and soldiers collected over two hundred thousand. When coffee beans were ready for harvest, the chief exchanged these beans for gourds, which the people badly needed. The coffee was then sold to Europeans for gold, thus allowing Haiti to build up a stable metal currency. Honoring that event in their history, the name for the unit of currency in Haiti is the *gourde*.

Gourd canteen used by California settlers in mid-19th century.
COLLECTION OF EUGENIA GWATHNEY

A crushed lime container from New Guinea, decorated with cowrie shells pressed into a tar-like substance. The lime is mixed with betelnut to create a slight stimulant.
COLLECTION OF
DICK AND BEANIE WEZELMAN

Because gourds played such an essential role in the daily life of all members of a culture, it is small wonder that they came to be used in religious and ceremonial rituals and were often believed to possess mystical properties. Evidence of this is found in the art and literature, the artifacts, and the religious ceremonies and rituals of many cultures. Frequently, medicine men and shaman used gourds as rattles, medicine bundles, altar pieces, and containers for holy relics. The Huichol Indians in Mexico believed that the spirits returned to the gourd when they visited the earth, so the interiors of gourds were elaborately decorated with sacred symbols using beads or colored yarns. In China, the gourd was believed to have supernatural powers like a crystal ball: by looking into a gourd, special people could not only read the future, but interpret the wishes of the gods.

Gourd cultivation, especially planting, was often surrounded in ritual and ceremony and reserved for specific individuals or groups of people in a community. But in one Caribbean island, the gourd was considered so sacred that only the shaman was allowed to plant, harvest, and use the fruit, and all other gourds that were not used by him were destroyed. As medicine bundles, sacred charm strings, masks, and rattles, gourds were an important part of the communication link between the visible and the invisible worlds.

Gourd elaborately decorated with shells and beads for use in special ceremonies in Benin, West Africa.
COLLECTION OF JEAN STRUTHERS

In China, special homes for pet crickets were created by growing a gourd in a mold and then capping it with an elaborate filigree top.
COLLECTION OF GINGER SUMMIT

Gourds were not only the vehicle by which man could address the spirits, but they provided the means through which the deities interacted with, and even created, the earth. The gourd plays a significant role in the origin myths of diverse peoples in Asia, Hawaii, Africa, and among the Indian tribes throughout the Americas. (Many fascinating examples of this are revealed in the book *The Gourd in Folk Literature*, by Eddie Wilson.) There are many examples of how the gourd, on being thrown down or split apart, became the heavens and the earth. According to one myth, the oceans, all the fish of the sea, and all of the creatures of the earth crawled out of a cracked gourd. Good spirits were believed to be transported to the earth within a gourd, and evil spirits were captured in the same vessel. Songs, chants, and prayers in every language pay homage to the wonderful mystery and power of this remarkable plant.

The types of decorations that have been used to embellish the gourd are as diverse as the applications and the cultures that employed them. Some gourds were left plain or were very crudely decorated. Others were covered with exquisite detail using such unusual techniques that people today are still unsure how the decoration was accomplished. With only simple tools and common objects, early craftsmen created impressive masterpieces of art and imagination.

The work of 122 contemporary gourd artists featured in this book demonstrates how today—as was true many centuries ago—the artists' own talent and cultural perspective, combined with the gourd's unique shapes and textures, create an astonishing marriage of art and nature. The 22 projects in the book afford you the opportunity to decorate gourds using dozens of techniques. And the more than 300 stunning gourds interspersed throughout the book are there to inspire you.

Chapter One

WHAT IS A GOURD?

Gourd Definition

One of the first questions a gourd lover is asked is "What is a gourd?" Unfortunately, that simple question does not have a simple answer.

In *Garden of Gourds* (Barber Press, 1937), botanist L.H. Bailey wrote a very broad definition of gourds: ..."members of the Cucurbitaceae family which produce a hard-shelled durable fruit grown for ornament, utensils, and general interest." In reality, the Cucurbitaceae family is very large, with more than 100 genera and 1,000 species. The primary characteristics that identify this family are having a tendril bearing vine with both male and female blossoms borne on the same vine, and producing a fruit that has an outer-shell covering (may dry to be soft or hard), with seeds imbedded in a pulp that is secured in three sections along the inside of the shell. Some of the more familiar members of this extensive family are pumpkins, squash, all melons, zucchinis, cucumbers—to name a few. Although these familiar fruits have firm outer shells when mature, most of them become soft when dry, or at least do not have a shell that is durable over time. At one time all members of the Cucurbitaceae family were loosely referred to with the all-inclusive term gourd, and this broad application is often found in popular literature today, especially when describing squash and pumpkins.

Several members of the Cucurbitacaea family specifically known as gourds—namely the wax gourd, bitter gourd, and hedgehog (teasel) gourd—don't dry with a durable shell. To complicate matters further, in many countries the term calabash is often used interchangeably with gourd. The term *calabash* is derived from the French word *calebasse* and the Spanish word *calabaza* and is used much more frequently in Africa and South and Middle America than the term gourd.

Adding even more confusion, the labels of gourd and calabash are both frequently used to describe the fruit of two trees—the *Crescentia cujete* and the *Crescentia alata*. Both of these trees grow in hot arid or tropical climates, generally Middle and South America, the Caribbean, and Florida. Their fruits are globular, ranging in size from baseballs to basketballs—usually round, but sometimes elongated. When dry the shell is very dense and will last indefinitely. Both the gourd vines and the calabash trees grow in the same areas, and their fruits have been, and continue to be, used for many of the same functions.

Naturalists and botanists have been very frustrated by the confusion in the terms gourd, calabash, calabaza, etc., applied to completely different referents, for it is often impossible to determine which fruit is being described. The suggestion has been made to designate calabash to refer to fruits that come from trees, and gourd to refer to the vine-borne fruits. History and cultures are difficult to change, however, and so the confusion continues.

Because tree gourds are rarely grown or found in the United States, this book focuses on only two members of the Cucurbitaceae family—the *Cucurbita pepo* (variety ovifera), a very long term to

The Calabash tree grows in Florida and the Caribbean, Middle and South America. The fruit dries to form a hard outer shell and has been used interchangeably with gourds in all of these areas.
PHOTO BY AMI DIALLO

describe the *ornamental* gourd group, and the *Lagenaria siceraria*, or *hardshell* variety. To keep things simple, these groups will be referred to by their familiar names—the ornamentals and the hardshells. In addition to many horticultural distinctions, the two varieties have several important differences that affect their use for craft purposes.

ORNAMENTAL GOURDS

The ornamental gourds are familiar reminders of autumn. One of Mother Nature's show-offs, they display a tremendous variety of shapes, surfaces, and colors, ranging from pale white to brilliant oranges, yellows, golds, and greens. Striped, spotted, and warty, these gourds are often varnished or polished to make them even more brilliant. But within a few months they usually mold and rot. Without the polish or varnish to clog their pores, many ornamental gourds dry naturally, losing their colorful epidermis, but still maintaining their distinctive shapes. After they are dried, they can be opened to reveal a thin shell that holds many seeds in a fibrous mass.

Within the ornamental variety, several subcategories are used to identify the gourds further. These categories tend to be largely descriptive, based on shape, size, and texture: nest egg, orange, pear, spoon, Holy Crown (also called crown-of-thorns, Ten Commandments, or finger), apple, bell, big bell, and depressa striata. Colors can vary within the categories from creamy white to yellow, orange, reddish orange, light, and dark green. These colors can be plain, striped, or mottled, and can even bisect a gourd. The surface texture is also difficult to predict: they may be warty, grooved, or smooth.

The size of the gourd is influenced by variety and growing conditions, although most tend to be under six inches in length or diameter; some are even smaller.

Ornamental gourds grow in a variety of shapes, sizes, and colors and are familiar harbingers of autumn in produce markets.

HARDSHELL GOURDS

In contrast, the hardshell gourds don't have the dramatic colors of the ornamental gourds. When harvested, they may be dark green to creamy white, with interesting variations of stripes or mottled spots. The wondrous quality of the hardshell variety, however, lies in the magical shapes that emerge as the plant grows. Through the ages, the plant has been hybridized both by the mutation that occurs naturally in the wild and by intentional planting by humans, to result in a fantastic variety of forms and sizes.

The categorical labels used to describe hardshell gourds generally refer to shape and size of the gourd, since the epidermal layer (which contains the color) molds as the gourd dries and is scraped off before the gourd is used. Most hardshells are smooth textured. Basically the hardshell gourds can be divided into four main classifications, based on general shape characteristics. Within each classification are many different subvarieties of gourds that share the same general shape but differ by size or by important horticultural or geographic distinctions. The wide range of names that have been applied to gourds is a natural outgrowth of their very antiquity, their extensive use throughout the world in diverse cultures, and the varied and unusual applications that have been found for this plant.

Gourds come in all shapes and sizes, which is a wonderful catalyst for an artist's creativity.

JOLEE SCHLEA
Kokopelli's Dance
PHOTO BY KIRK SCHLEA

When they are mature, hardshell gourds can vary from ivory to dark green, with mottled patterns. They are especially prized for their fantastic shapes and sizes.

A WORD ABOUT LUFFAS

The luffa sponge gourd, a member of the cucurbitacaea family, may be more closely related to the cucumber than the hardshell lagenaria. Like all its family relatives, it grows on a luxurious vine and produces delicate pale yellow blossoms 50 to 60 days after planting. Luffa plants thrive best when grown on a trellis—the fruit can grow up to 2 feet in length and weigh up to 5 pounds. Some cultures, particularly in Asia, harvest luffas for food while they are small and green. But in much of the world the luffa is valued for its spongy interior. After it has been harvested and dried, the thin outer shell can be soaked and peeled away, leaving a cylindrical sponge housing hundreds of seeds. The sponge is extremely durable and has been used throughout the world for a multitude of purposes including packing material, padding for pillows, mattresses, and saddles, lining for pith helmets, material for construction of slippers and mats, even as an oil filter on diesel engines.

Perhaps the most familiar use is as a scrubbing material; many people know this plant as the "dishrag" plant. Luffas have been used to scrub everything from delicate skin to dishes, windows and floors, cars and boats. Luffas were used in ancient Egypt and have been used medicinally in cultures throughout the middle and far East. (See Supply Sources on page 142.)

Naming Gourds

The American Gourd Society (AGS) has attempted to standardize the names of the more familiar shapes, to facilitate communication between growers, crafters, and the general public. For a more complete description of gourd types, contact the AGS (See Supply Sources on page 142 for address).

Many gourd growers are interested in preserving the true identity of specific shapes, sizes, and horticultural characteristics of the individual types of hardshell gourd, and in creating and maintaining reliable and predictable seeds. However, in addition to the genetic inheritance contained within the seed, the size and shape of the fruit can be greatly affected by soil and weather conditions. As a result, there is often variability in the shapes and sizes produced within each specific category listed above. For the gourd artist and crafts person, this variety produces much of the pleasure of the plant.

Basket Type

These gourds are generally round and either have no neck or are somewhat tapered toward the stem end of the body. Some of the more familiar shapes are:

CANNONBALL

4"– 5" diameter

BASKETBALL

10" diameter

Bottle Type

These gourds generally have a base bulb and a neck at the stem end. There may be a bulb in the neck, with a constriction, or waist, separating the two bulbs. Some popular shapes are:

MINIATURE BOTTLE

4"– 6" height

MARTIN HOUSE

10"– 14" height

Dipper Type

These gourds have a bulb at the blossom end of the gourd with a long thin neck extending to the stem end. The stem may be straight or curved, depending on if they are grown on the ground or on a trellis.

SHORT-HANDLED DIPPER

up to 6" handle

MID-SIZE DIPPER

Trough/Siphon/Snake

These gourds are generally long with no distinct bulb.

BANANA

7"– 10" length

SNAKE

2'– 3' length

NOTE: MEASUREMENTS ARE APPROXIMATE AND VARY WITHIN EACH TYPE

CCO BOX

ght

CANTEEN

6" height

BUSHEL BASKET

12"– 18" height

JAPANESE BASKET

ACOMA/ HOPI RATTLE

Small canteen with character-istic sickle scar on bottom.

UIN OR POWDERHORN

6" height

INDONESIAN

6" height

LUMP-IN-NECK

HARDSHELL WARTIE

CHINESE BOTTLE

10"– 14" height

A-LONG HANDLED R

length

CLUB

MARANKA

CLUB

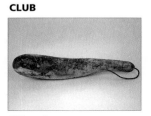

2' length

ZUCCA

2'– 3' length

Ornamental gourds come in beautiful colors and many different shapes.

Horticulture

Growing gourds is very similar to growing any of their relatives in the cucurbit family. With minimal effort, the casual gardener will be rewarded with a nice crop of interesting and varied gourds, both large and small. However, there are many actions that can be taken to insure a healthy, abundant, and predictable crop.

THE GOURD FACTORY, LINDEN, CALIFORNIA

Gourds can be grown in containers and supported on trellises to save space. Ornamental gourds and mini-hardshell gourds are the most suitable choices for this type of gardening.

GARDEN OF MARLENE TATE
PHOTO BY GINGER SUMMIT

SEED SELECTION

When you decide to grow gourds, the first consideration is seed selection. Obviously, healthy and productive gourd plants must start from healthy seeds or from seeds that have come from last season's sturdiest gourds. Gourds are hybrids. Because each seed within a gourd has been fertilized by a different pollen grain, it is impossible to predict what the resulting gourd will be like unless special care has been taken in the pollination of the gourd plant for many past generations. Although gourds of a particular variety share many characteristics, each gourd has its own individuality.

Many specialty seed and nursery companies are able to provide seeds that match the customer's interest in gourds of a particular size and shape. Experienced gourd growers are careful to raise single varieties of gourds spaced far from other varieties to reduce the risk of cross-pollination.

If you plan to save certain gourds for seeds, don't let the gourds freeze or the seeds will not germinate. Harvest them as soon as the vines die back and take the gourds indoors to dry. Carefully select the largest seeds from robust gourds and store the seeds in tightly sealed containers in the refrigerator. Baby-food jars and small plastic film canisters work well. Mark the container with the date, variety, and any other information that will be useful at planting time. Seeds can be stored in this manner for up to four years. If you haven't taken special care in the pollination of the gourds, interesting hybrid shapes will eventually emerge from the seeds.

GROWING ORNAMENTAL GOURDS

The easiest gourd to grow is the ornamental. It can be grown very successfully in a container or on a trellis or fence. The requirements are simple: 1) fertilized soil that is enriched occasionally throughout the growing season, 2) regular watering, and 3) a warm sunny location. Plant the seeds about 1-1/2 inches deep, either in rows or hills or in a container. If you plant them in hills, place up to eight seeds in hillocks spaced eight to ten feet apart. If you are planting in rows, the rows should be at least eight feet apart. With care you will be rewarded in about 100 days with a bounty of small decorative gourds that can be harvested soon after they reach maturity. Seed packets that contain a variety of shapes and colors of ornamental gourds can be purchased at most garden supply stores. If you want specific shapes, contact the seed sources listed on page 142.

GROWING HARDSHELL GOURDS

The hardshell gourds, available in many more choices of shapes and sizes than the ornamentals, also need the three elements listed above. In addition, the vigorous vining hardshell requires plenty of growing room and at least 130 days of full sun, or temperatures above 80 degrees Fahrenheit for 50 days, between the last spring frost and the first fall frost. If you live in an area with a shorter growing season, you can start the plants indoors and transplant when danger the of frost is past. Most gardening books describe this process. Planting instructions for hardshells are the same as for ornamentals, described above.

SOIL AND FERTILIZER

To grow healthy ornamentals and hardshell gourds, fertilize the soil well, especially when the seeds are first planted. Initially, the soil should be rich in phosphorus, potassium, and nitrogen. Add well-rotted manure and a good commercial fertilizer (10-10-10) to the area where the seeds will be planted. Bonemeal is a good source of additional potassium. The first two months of plant growth are spent developing a healthy root system. Therefore, during this time the plant must have water and nitrogen, even though the plant appears to be growing slowly. Apply fertilizers such as fish emulsion periodically during the growing season to promote healthy vines.

As the fruit begins to set, however, nitrogen-rich fertilizer should be eliminated because vigorous leaf growth is no longer necessary. Purchase one of the nitrogen-free fertilizers sold in nurseries and apply it monthly to promote vigorous gourd fruit growth.

WATER

Adequate watering is essential to healthy gourd development. Seeds should be kept moist until the young plants begin to emerge from the ground. As roots become established and leaves appear, water the seedlings every other day. Once you have thinned the plants, reduce the watering to one to two deep soakings weekly, taking care not to get the leaves wet. Maintain this watering schedule throughout the season until the plants are approaching maturity in the early fall; then you can stop watering them.

THINNING AND PRUNING

When the plants have developed several leaves and it's apparent which seedlings are vigorous, thin the hills to two to three seedlings apiece. Within eight to ten weeks from planting, the primary vine of the gourd plant may be approximately ten feet long and may be developing lateral branches. Pinch off the end of the primary vine to force more growth in the lateral branches. The male flowers of the gourd plant blossom on the main vine stem, and the female blossoms are located on the lateral branches. Because the female flowers produce the fruit, or the gourd, it is important to encourage a maximum growth along the laterals. You can also prune the first lateral branches when they reach a length of four to six feet to increase growth in the secondary laterals.

Hardshell gourds require a great deal of space. Vines can grow up to 100 feet in length.

GARDEN OF MARLENE TATE

PHOTO BY GINGER SUMMIT

MAKING A TRELLIS

The vines of healthy plants grow extremely rapidly. In their search for adequate space and sunshine, the vines will invade any neighboring area, including nearby trees. It's a good idea to build a trellis or fence to support the vine. This strategy is useful for many reasons: gourd leaves should not get wet frequently because this encourages powdery mildew and other diseases. By raising the vines on a trellis, the roots can be watered thoroughly and the leaves kept dry. Leaves and fruit suspended in the air are less susceptible to bugs, insects, and diseases that may be in or on the ground. Also, fruits that grow on a trellis tend to be more symmetrical and blemish-free than fruit that matures on the ground. A trellis designed to support gourds must be very sturdy. The healthy vines will completely cover the trellis itself, grabbing for support with very tightly curled tendrils. Flimsy trellises can be broken or stretched apart by the weight and strength of these vines. Also, the gourd fruit is very heavy. Particularly on prolific vines, the cumulative weight of vines and many gourds is substantial. When designing or planning for above-ground support, select materials that are strong and designs that provide maximum support. Several options are available: PVC pipe, tent poles, two-by-four-foot frames, old ladders, heavy fencing, to name a few.

GROWING ON THE GROUND

When gourds are grown on the ground, it's important to lightly dust them with insecticide to prevent insects from attacking the vulnerable young gourds. Many people recommend placing a slight support under the gourd. This can range from extra straw or mulch, a plastic bag or sheet, a piece of cardboard or board, or even a wooden pallet. By raising the gourd off the ground, you minimize the rot, fungus, and mildew that can affect a plant grown on a damp surface.

POLLINATION

The difference between the ornamental and hardshell gourds becomes most apparent as the gourd plants begin to flower. The ornamental vine produces lovely large golden yellow flowers that nestle among the green leaves. The hardshell plants produce beautiful lacy white flowers that rise above the green leaf carpet on delicate stalks.

All gourd plants produce both male and female flowers on a single vine, but only the female has a prominent bulge immediately below the flower, which, if fertilized, will eventually become a gourd. The male flower is usually found on the primary vine and has a slightly longer stalk that stands upright above the leaves. The female plant is found on the lateral branches and often is closer to the stalk on a shorter stem.

As the gourds begin to mature, thin them in order to encourage larger growth in the remaining fruits. By placing the young gourd upright or on its side, it is possible to influence the shape and to encourage an even or flat bottom that will allow the gourd to stand securely when it is dry. Long gourds, such as the snake or long-handled dippers, can be trained by tying them with strips of rags or nylon stockings to create the desired shapes and angles. If left to mature on the ground, these gourds often assume very twisted shapes.

Gourds on the vine can be very heavy and require a sturdy trellis. This one built by Glenn Burkhalter will support gourds for years.
PHOTO BY GLENN BURKHALTER

DISEASES AND PESTS

Gourds are subject to the same diseases and pests that attack melons, squash, and cucumbers. By planting the gourds in a different location each year, the problem of diseases and pests is automatically reduced substantially. Some of the common problems include powdery mildew, melon aphid, striped cucumber beetle, bacterial wilt, and anthracnose. If any of these problems occur on your gourd plants, consult your local nursery or farm extension expert for treatment recommendations.

HARVESTING THE GOURDS

When the stem of an ornamental gourd appears brown and the tendrils next to the fruit are dry, the fully grown gourd can be picked; the vine and remaining gourds will continue to grow. If colored ornamental gourds are left on the vine, the colors will fade in the sunlight. When removing the gourd, it's important to leave a portion of the stem, an inch if possible, attached to the gourd.

Hardshell gourds must be handled differently. These gourds should not be harvested until autumn when the entire vine has dried and turned brown. Gourds that set late in the summer may not have had time to mature and will eventually wither. You can determine if the gourd is fully mature by pushing at the base of the stem: the gourd will feel firm and solid to the touch. It will vary in color from dark green to creamy white and be covered with a waxy coating. Now the gourd enters a new phase—that of curing. This process may take from several weeks to many months, occasionally up to a year. At the start of curing, the gourd—even though mature—is still fragile. Rough handling, which can bruise or scratch the shell, may so weaken the gourd that it will rot rather than harden.

Many gardeners recommend leaving the gourds on the vine until they have had a chance to dry at least partially. However, if the gourd vines have been infected with any disease, carefully remove all gourds from the fields and store them in a well-ventilated area off the ground and preferably not touching each other. The dried vines should be burned off, if possible, or at least gathered and removed from the area of cultivation. Any imperfect gourds that you don't harvest should be removed so they don't become homes to insects, rodents, or disease.

All other gourds can safely be left outside to dry. Turn the gourds periodically (once a week) to insure even drying and to prevent the possibility of the underside getting soft and then rotting.

Long-handled dipper gourd being shaped by wrapping and tying with a cord.

GARDEN OF JIM STORY   PHOTOS BY JIM STORY

The gourd in the picture above, after it was harvested, dried, and scraped.

GROWN BY JIM STORY
PHOTO BY JIM STORY

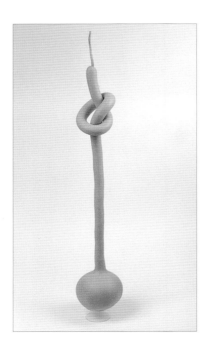

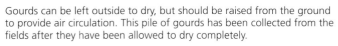

Gourds can be left outside to dry, but should be raised from the ground to provide air circulation. This pile of gourds has been collected from the fields after they have been allowed to dry completely.

THE GOURD FACTORY, LINDEN, CALIFORNIA

Chapter Two

GENERAL PROCESSES

Curing and Cleaning the Exterior

CURING FRESHLY HARVESTED MATURE GOURDS

When gourds have matured thoroughly on the vine, the shell is firm to the touch and is covered with a thin protective waxy epidermis, or skin. The skins of ornamental gourds have bright and varied colors, including yellows, oranges, and greens in sometimes fascinating patterns and combinations. Hardshell gourds are less colorful but also have interesting patterns of greens and ivory. Unfortunately, the colors that are so beautiful in the fall are contained in the epidermis, which fades and eventually is shed as the gourd cures. Even though the shell is firm, it's still somewhat fragile and should be handled carefully so as not to bruise, nick, or scratch the protective skin.

At the time of harvest, the gourd is composed of 90 percent water. Curing is the process of evaporation as all the interior water slowly leaches out through the porous woody outer shell and eventually dries on the gourd surface. The drying time for freshly harvested gourds varies from six weeks to more than a year depending on the type of gourd, its size, the thickness of its shell, and the weather conditions. It's hard to estimate accurately, because some small ornamental gourds with thin shells may take several months to dry, and certain hardshell gourds will dry in a much shorter time.

Sometimes it's difficult to tell if a gourd is completely dry, although experience will give you many clues. The shell becomes a light tan/brown shade (under the molded epidermis) and the seeds usually will rattle. The gourd will feel relatively light when picked up. Again, however, there is variability within each of these

CAROL ANN JOHNSON
A pattern was scratched in the epidermis of this gourd while still green. When dried, the epidermis became a cream-colored waxy coating on the rest of the gourd.

features. Some gourds have very thick and dense shells and even when dry are heavy relative to their size when compared to other similar sized gourds. Sometimes the pulp has dried to form a fibrous mat that sticks to the inside of the gourd, encasing the seeds so that they don't loosen and rattle against the dry shell. Also, the color tone of the gourd may vary from creamy tan to a relatively dark shade of brown. Experience provides the best basis for judgment as to when a gourd is dry.

Mature healthy gourds can be left outside to dry even in freezing weather; the alternate freezing and thawing help to loosen the epidermal skin and ease the eventual cleaning job. Whether left outside or brought under cover, the gourd should be well ventilated and, preferably, stored off the ground. As the water evaporates and dries on the gourd surface, it forms a mold on the exterior shell.

SCRAPING THE GOURD EPIDERMIS

If you are able to obtain a green or fresh gourd soon after it's harvested in the fall, you can prevent mold from forming on the surface by frequently wiping it with a mild solution of household disinfectant during the long drying process. The result will be a dried gourd with a more evenly toned surface.

Another way to hasten the drying process requires a bit more time and effort. Soon after harvesting, the outer skin of the hardshell gourd begins to change color from green to a creamy white and begins to loosen. By testing with your fingernail at the base of the stem, you can determine when the skin is beginning to soften. At this stage, you can remove the skin fairly easily by scraping it with a dull kitchen knife or scraper edge. A gourd that has been scraped will dry faster, but is susceptible to mold or fungus; store it in a well-ventilated area and wipe it frequently with a cloth that has been soaked in a mild solution of water and disinfectant. This will remove the evaporated moisture and prevent mold buildup. The dried gourd that results from this care has a very pale surface, free of the mottled marblings that often distinguish gourds dried naturally.

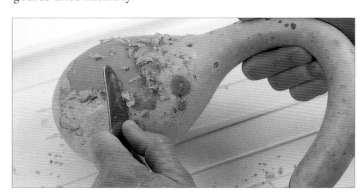

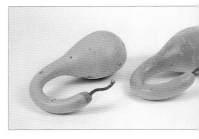

Pictured to the right is a grouping of the same three gourds, photographed over a four month period, to demonstrate the changes that occur during curing. The gourd on the left was scraped; the middle gourd was wiped with bleach; the gourd on the right was untouched.

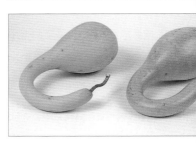

OTHER WAYS TO HASTEN DRYING

Ancient cultures around the world devised many different methods to hasten the drying period or ease the cleaning process. One such method was to cut off the end of the green gourd and scoop out some of the pulp. The shell was then filled with water, either salt or fresh, and the gourd was left alone for up to one month. The pulp would eventually soften and become slightly gelatinous, at which point it was easily washed away. The shell was then placed in the sun or by a fire to dry, which caused it to dry fairly rapidly.

This method works well with thick-shelled gourds. If you try it, be sure—while the shell is drying—to examine it periodically and remove all traces of mold as it forms. The drying time for the shell will vary and depends on where it is stored and the density of the individual shell.

Other methods have been suggested to hasten the drying process, such as poking holes in the gourd or storing it in a warm area. These methods are not recommended; gourds that are punctured will attract mold or fungus and are more likely to decay rather than harden.

PRESERVING THE COLOR OF ORNAMENTAL GOURDS

The above discussion on drying and washing applies to all hardshell gourds and to many ornamental varieties. However, some ornamentals will never dry with a permanent woody shell, and even with care, they will eventually lose their lovely color and rot. A bulletin available from the American Gourd Society suggests a process that can preserve the color for up to two years (see the source list on page 142).

When most small ornamental gourds are allowed to dry naturally, they lose their colorful exterior skin and become the light brown tones of the hardshell varieties. The woody shell is thin, however, and should be handled with care.

LEAVING THE MOLD ON THE GOURDS

Before you clean a gourd surface, take a close look at the interesting patterns created by the mold and dried outer skin. Often you will find an unusual texture and pattern on the smooth surface that you can incorporate into the final design. If you do decide to leave some of the gourd shell "au naturel," protect the surface with several coats of shellac, varnish, or fixative spray to prevent the mold from eventually flaking off or from being picked away by well-intentioned viewers.

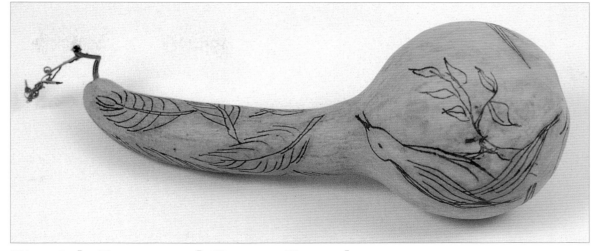

Scratch-Engraved Green Gourd

Instead of removing the entire epidermis of a green gourd, you can carve designs in it using a stencil or film line cutter.

WHAT YOU NEED

> Green gourd
> Sharp pencil
> Stencil or film line cutter
>   (available in art and
>   craft stores)
> Plastic gloves
> Wood stain or leather dye
> Soft cloth
> Dull kitchen knife

WHAT YOU DO

1. Draw a design on the epidermis of the gourd with a pencil. Scratch along the lines with the stencil or film line cutter, removing the epidermis as you cut. Be careful not to scratch into the actual gourd shell (Photo 1).

2. Brush or wipe the designed areas with wood stain or leather dye, making sure that the design is thoroughly colored (Photo 2). Wipe off the excess dye or stain.

3. Leave the epidermis on the gourd to dry naturally or scrape it off with the kitchen knife after the stained or dyed design is completely dry (Photo 3).

4. The finished gourd shows how the waxy epidermis protected the gourd shell: only the scraped lines retain the color.

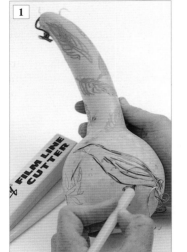

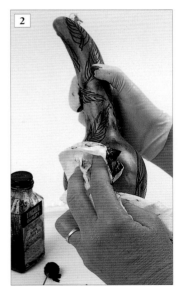

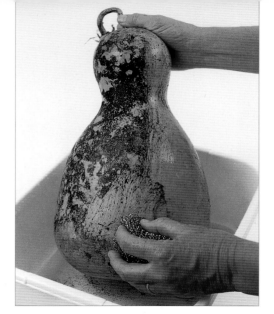

CLEANING METHODS

There are several ways to clean the mold from gourds that have been allowed to dry without special care. While the job is messy, it is not difficult. Be sure to clean the stems, too; they also have exterior skin that molds. To enhance the final project, treat the stem the same way you treat the gourd. Here are six procedures for cleaning gourds.

• Soak the gourds in a tub of water into which you have mixed a small amount of bleach or disinfectant. Because dry gourds float, you will need to cover them with a weight or put them in a burlap bag weighted down with a brick; this will insure that the gourds are thoroughly and completely covered with water. After a length of time—from 15 minutes to several hours, depending on the condition of the gourd—scrub off the mold with a plastic or metal kitchen scrubbing pad or a stiff natural brush. (Copper scouring pads are less abrasive than other metal pads and do not scratch the surface. See photo left.) Stubborn spots can be scraped off with a dull knife or file.

• Wrap the gourd in a wet towel and set it in the sun for several hours to soften the mold. Remove the mold with a rough scrub pad or brush.

• Place moldy gourds or gourds that have been loosely wrapped in towels in a large plastic garbage bag. Add some water and a small amount of detergent and tightly secure the bag. Leave the bagged gourds in the sun for several hours, carefully rolling the bag over from time to time. A black or dark colored bag will absorb more energy from the sun and will heat both the water and the gourds. This process effectively steam-soaks the mold, which then can usually be scraped off quite easily.

• Scrape off stubborn mold spots with a kitchen knife blade or file. (Be careful not to scratch the surface of the gourd.) A wire brush or very stiff scrub brush is useful for cleaning warty gourds.

• If you are going to paint or seal the gourd prior to decorating it, you can remove mold spots by lightly rubbing the gourd with sandpaper or steel wool. Some hardware stores carry a coarse drywall sanding screen, which is also useful. However, if you plan to stain or dye the gourd, sandpaper may leave scratches on the surface that will affect the appearance of the added color.

• Sometimes dried gourds have relatively little exterior mold; the epidermis becomes a waxy cream-color skin that firmly coats the gourds. Usually this is the result of gourds that have been dried indoors or in a warm condition. Although this waxy coating is very pretty and may remain permanently and indefinitely on a gourd surface, it does form a barrier to any type of paint or surface embellishment. Try using this skin like a wax resist: scrape away portions of the skin and stain or dye the rest. If you want to remove the skin from the entire shell, simply soak it for several hours and it should easily rub off.

MAURICE GOSDEN
Stain and varnish were painted over the dried epidermis of this gourd to preserve the interesting texture and color pattern.

COLLECTION OF CHRIS HOBACK

GAYE COOK
A gourd does not have to be scraped or cleaned. If you want to save the pattern of the molded epidermis, be sure to varnish it so that it does not flake off.

Cutting and Cleaning the Interior

CUTTING THE GOURD SHELL

Many different tools are suitable for cutting a hardshell gourd. The choice depends on the type of cut you wish to make, the surface thickness of the gourd, and your access to tools. Hand tools, power hobby tools, and sharp knives can all be used in different types of cutting situations.

When using any kind of saw, the first challenge is to hold the gourd in a stable position. Brace it on a solid surface, preferably wedged in a corner where you can hold the gourd firmly in place. A rubber or nonskid surface can help to keep it from slipping and sliding. We found that a 2-inch (5.1 cm) foam pad works best to cushion and secure the gourd on a flat surface. Many artists hold the gourd against their body or in their lap when cutting. This is fine when you are using hand tools but is not safe when using power tools. You can also grip the gourd with a nonslip material; a rubberized work glove or a thin rubber mat works well.

HAND TOOLS

The easiest type of cut is one that simply removes the top or end portion of the gourd straight across, dividing the gourd into one or two container portions. You can use any type of wood saw. The tooth of the saw blade should be reasonably fine so that it doesn't rip or crack a soft or thin gourd shell.

More frequently you will want to make an irregular opening or cut around the circumference of the gourd.

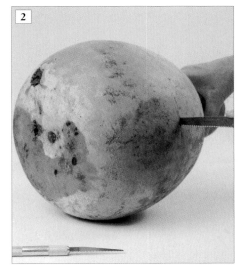

- To do this, sketch the cutting line lightly on the gourd surface with a pencil or chalk (Photo 1). If you want a perfectly level cut around the wide part of the body, you can construct a brace to hold a pencil at a given height and slowly rotate the gourd against the pencil tip.

- Once you have determined where the cut will be, make a slit along the pencil line with a sharp knife (Photo 2).

- Insert a keyhole saw or hobby saw into the slit and slowly cut around the line you have drawn (Photo 3).

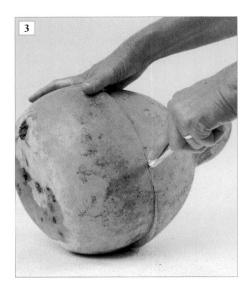

POWER TOOLS

Another option is to use a small motorized cutting tool, such as those made by Dremel, Foredom, Minicraft, or Micro-Mark. Along with a wide assortment of interchangeable tips, these tools have several diameters of round saw blades that effectively turn the tool into a tiny circular saw. These blades are suitable only for straight cuts, however, since they will bind if the cutting line becomes curved.

Small hand-held power jigsaws designed for the hobbyist, such as those made by Minicraft or Micro-Mark, are excellent tools. Draw the cutting line on the gourd shell and make a slit with a sharp knife for the saw blade to enter. Before you turn on the power, make sure that the saw is resting firmly against the shell (otherwise it may cause the shell to bounce and crack when the blade begins to pulse). With the gourd securely braced against a solid surface, you can cut even very curved lines with ease.

SAFETY PRECAUTIONS

SAFETY PRECAUTIONS

The gourd's interior pulp and the dust created by scraping or sanding the gourd are toxic and irritating for some people. Complaints include puffy eyes and constricted nasal passages and occasionally difficulty in breathing. Many people describe a strange taste in their mouth as they clean and scrape gourds. Therefore, take the following precautions when cleaning gourds.

- Do all the cleaning outside to allow for maximum ventilation. The cleaning process is rather messy, so an added bonus to working outdoors is that you will keep gourd dust and debris out of your work space.

- Wear a dust mask. These are available at a very reasonable cost from most hardware stores and pharmacies. A dusk mask is lightweight and easy to wear. For more complete protection, many styles of air filtering masks are available. Some simply cover the face and are tied around the head, protecting nose, eyes, and mouth while filtering the air that is breathed. More elaborate masks can be purchased that provide a separate air supply. Look for these products in hardware stores and craft catalogs.

- Use a fan to blow away noxious dust. You can also use a shop vacuum hose with a good filter to suck in the dust as the gourd is cleaned.

- To reduce dust particles, partially fill the gourd with water or spray the gourd interior with water and scrape out only the wet pulp and seeds. Try some of the alternative methods of cleaning recommended on pages 26 and 30.

- People with sensitive skin or those allergic to dust may want to wear plastic or rubber gloves when cleaning gourds.

CLEANING THE INTERIOR

Once an opening is made in the gourd shell, you can remove the interior pulp and seeds using a variety of tools. You can often take out much of the material by hand. Save the seeds for planting if the gourd has a shape and shell that are attractive or useful to you. Save the pulp to make paper or to add to your compost.

In search of the perfect tool, people improvise with tools and equipment borrowed from the kitchen drawer, hobby box, or junk yard. Unfortunately, gourds are as varied on the inside as on the outside, and you will probably want to build up a collection of tools to meet all the different cleaning needs. The following list includes some of the more familiar tools that have been used frequently and successfully.

- Grapefruit spoon, ice cream scoop, or old metal kitchen spoon whose edges have been sharpened and serrated with a file.

- Melon baller (good for smaller gourds and spaces with very curved interiors)

- Plastic and metal pot scrapers

- Assorted shapes and sizes of wood chisels and files.

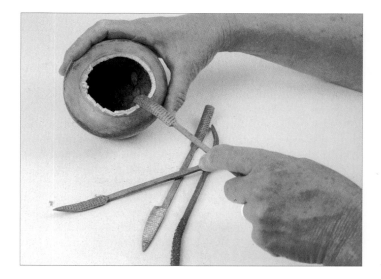

- Tools used by ceramic artists to smooth or texture clay surfaces.

- Wire brushes that can be attached to a power drill. If the gourd is deep, you can get an extension that allows the wire brush to reach into more difficult spaces. Be careful not to apply too much pressure so that the brush cuts through the gourd shell. Some shells have softer sections, and because wire brushes can be very abrasive, you may end up with a bumpy and irregular surface. If used only on selected gourds with thick and evenly dense shells, however, this tool is very useful.

- Sanding discs with flexible rubber backing that can be attached to power sanders. This tool is very useful for smoothing the interior of gourd trays, dishes, and open shallow bowls.

- Pliers for cutting off the inside nipple.

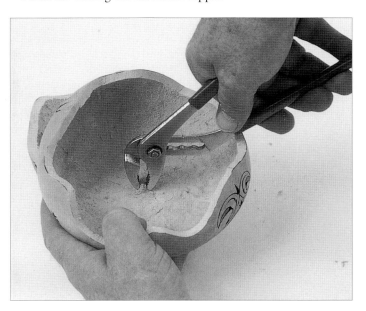

- Homemade sharpened tools for reaching into thin and deep gourds. To reach into the narrow portions of some gourds, such as the snake or dipper handle, tools can be made of bent wire or long-handled barbecue forks. Another tool can be made by inserting a sturdy wire (such as a coat hanger) into a short length of PVC pipe. The length of wire and the length of pipe will depend on the shape and size of the gourd to be cleaned. Bend one end of the wire into a circle (from the diameter of a nickel to that of a quarter) and roughen the edges with a file to provide an abrasive edge. Insert the wire through the pipe and bend the other end into two right angles to form a handle; the uppermost portion can be padded with tape to allow for a better gripping surface.

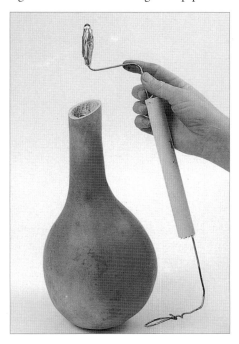

- Insert the tool into the narrow gourd. Hold the PVC pipe steady with one hand and turn the handle with the other; the circular end of the wire will scrape and loosen the pulp in the interior.

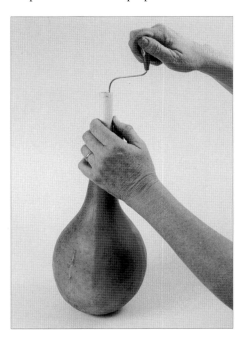

HOW CLEAN IS CLEAN?

Once the pulp and seeds have been scraped free, the interior can be further smoothed with a metal scouring pad, a sanding fabric, or sandpaper.

How thoroughly to clean the interior will depend on your own personal preferences and on the uses of the finished product. Minimal cleaning is sufficient if you are making a purely decorative container, particularly one with a small opening or with an interior that will eventually be covered, colored, or stained. If the opening is large, the aesthetic value of the piece is greatly enhanced by a carefully cleaned and smooth interior. When gourds are intended for use as containers, and especially when they will be used with foods, it's very important to thoroughly clean and smooth the interior.

ALTERNATIVE METHODS FOR CLEANING THE INTERIOR

Through the centuries and around the world, different cultures found effective and often simple ways to clean gourd interiors. People in locations as diverse as Africa and New Zealand cut the tops off green gourds and filled them with water. After several weeks, the interior pulp turned into a very soft mush and was easy to pour out and scrape from the sides. The gourd shell was then allowed to complete its drying either in the sun or next to a fire. Other tribes in Africa, North and South America allowed the gourd to completely dry first and then cut an opening in the shell. The gourd was filled with water, either salt or fresh (depending on culture and location), allowed to stand until the pulp was completely softened and mushy, and was then scraped clean with a shell or smooth stone. This method was particularly effective for long narrow containers such as those used by the Masai in Kenya to collect blood from cows. After most of the pulp and seeds were removed, the gourd was again filled with water and rough gravel, and then shaken to completely clean and scour the interior. Once cleaned in this manner, the gourd shell was allowed to dry naturally.

These methods of cleaning are very effective and useful alternatives for the crafter today who wants to avoid contact with gourd dust. Here are some points to keep in mind.

• This is not a good method if you are in a hurry: The interior needs to soak for up to one month to completely soften the pulp. If the interior is cleaned right after water is put in, the gourd dust will be reduced, but the pulp may stick to the gourd shell. If the water is left in the gourd for several days or up to a week, the pulp begins to soften and is much easier to pull away from the shell. If the water is left in the shell for up to one month, the pulp becomes very mushy; at this point it is very simple to pour it out and gently scrape the sides of the gourd clean.

• When the gourd shell is soaked in water, it may become slightly soft and bloated. When scraping the pulp, you may accidentally poke a hole through a thin shell. Therefore, clean carefully!

• The gourd shell will take several days, at least, to become thoroughly dry, before any craft work can be started. If mold begins to form while the shell is drying, clean it immediately with mild bleach.

RIMONA GALE
Sometimes the dried pulp forms a satin-like covering over the interior surface of the gourd. You may want to leave it just as it is.

Leaf Bowl

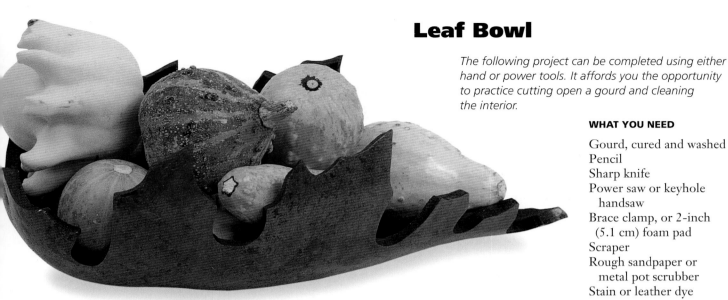

The following project can be completed using either hand or power tools. It affords you the opportunity to practice cutting open a gourd and cleaning the interior.

WHAT YOU NEED

Gourd, cured and washed
Pencil
Sharp knife
Power saw or keyhole
   handsaw
Brace clamp, or 2-inch
   (5.1 cm) foam pad
Scraper
Rough sandpaper or
   metal pot scrubber
Stain or leather dye
Varnish

WHAT YOU DO

1. Draw the leaf design onto the gourd with a pencil (Photo 1).

2. Make an incision in the gourd shell with a sharp knife. Then, use a small hobby knife, key-hole handsaw, or power saw to cut along the pencil line (Photo 2).

3. If you use a power tool, make sure the gourd is secure on the work surface. The gourd clamp shown in photo 3 is made from four pieces of wood and three spring hinges and is available through West Mountain Gourd Farm, listed in Supply Sources on page 142.

4. Once you have cut open the gourd along the pencil line, loosen and remove as much pulp as possible by hand (Photo 4).

5. Use a scraper to clean the rest of the pulp from the sides of the gourd. Here we used a wire brush attachment on an electric drill. If the gourd shell is soft in any portion, the wire brush may gouge too deeply. Be sure to proceed slowly and even-ly over the entire interior (Photo 5).

6. Remove as much of the soft interior as de-sired by sanding the interior with rough sand-paper or a metal pot scrubber.

7. Finish the inside and the outside of the bowl with stain or leather dye (see photo top). Var-nish to seal the surfaces before using.

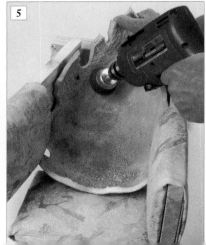

Ornamental Gourd Flowers

The ornamental gourd usually has a thin shell that you can easily cut with a craft knife. Experiment with different tools and various ornamentals to determine which are best for cutting; some shells may be slightly more dense than others. The craft knife comes with a variety of blade shapes, so experiment until you find the one that is most useful for your own style.

WHAT YOU NEED

10 ornamental gourds, cured and washed
Bowl of water
Craft knife
Sharp scissors or garden shears
Stains or acrylic paints
Craft glue
Natural materials, such as poppy and caraway seeds, peppercorns, or tiny dried flowers
10 lengths of heavy-gauge floral wire

WHAT YOU DO

1. Soak the gourds in water for a few minutes to soften the shell. Cut each gourd in half with a craft knife and discard the fibrous pulp. Turn each half upside down on a flat surface and cut the shell into segments by making slits along its sides (Photo 1).

2. Use a sharp pair of scissors or shears to shape the segments into petals (Photo 2).

3. When the gourd is dry, stain or paint the flowers (Photo 3).

4. When the stain or paint is dry, glue the natural materials onto the centers of the flowers. Glue on a stem of floral wire and arrange the flowers in a gourd vase.

Note of thanks: *This project was influenced by Eva Pawlak.*

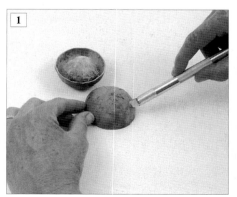

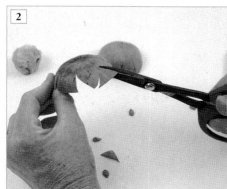

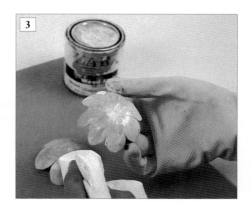

Exterior Finishes

Is a finish really necessary on the outside of a decorated gourd? The natural gourd surface is smooth and has nice coloration; if you have carved, cut, or woodburned the gourd, its natural colors may look especially attractive. Through the ages, gourds have been left untreated; interaction with the atmosphere, combined with the natural skin oils of people handling the gourds, can give them a soft patina.

However, because the gourd surface is porous, it will absorb anything that is unintentionally spilled or rubbed on it. What's more, the surface may become dry and brittle due to exposure to the natural atmosphere. If left in the sun, the natural shades of the gourd will bleach and the surface skin may become slightly pithy or porous. If left out in the weather, the gourd shell may also swell and bloat and possibly develop mildew or rot, especially if there are cracks or holes in the gourd. The good news is that there are many ways you can finish a gourd's exterior, both to protect it and to enhance its naturally beautiful colors and textures.

ROBIN ANN HUNTER
This gourd has been protected with multiple coats of high-gloss varnish to create a shiny rich luster that contrasts dramatically with the natural gourd mosaic.

SUSAN MCGANN
Peace
PHOTO BY KEN WAGNER

WAXES AND POLISHES

Waxes designed for shoes, leather, wood furniture, and floors provide an excellent and popular finish for gourds. Paste waxes come in a range of hardness, depending on the original uses for which they were designed. Waxes intended for outside use, on painted or metal surfaces (such as cars and boats), are usually very hard and are not recommended for the porous surface of the gourd. Floor paste wax is slightly softer and can be rubbed into the gourd surface and buffed to a very bright sheen. Because floor wax is designed to withstand traffic and surface spills, it will provide a relatively durable and protective coating for a gourd. Liquid floor wax penetrates the gourd shell more than paste wax and once dry buffs up to a sheen. Floor waxes are formulated to be neutral in color, ranging from no color at all to a slight yellowing effect (undesirable on a floor surface but acceptable on many gourds).

Waxes and polishes designed for wood and leather furniture contain less wax than products designed for the floor and will not provide the same degree of sheen. However, they are still desirable for use on gourds because they fill in the pores of the shell and provide some protection against light handling.

Furniture polish is often available in several shades of brown, intended to disguise or eliminate scratches and watermarks from flat furniture surfaces. These brown shades can produce lovely effects on gourds and enhance the natural patterns of the shell. However, if the gourd has soft or porous sections, it may absorb the tints of the polish unevenly.

Waxes designed for shoes are available in many colors, from the familiar shades of brown, white, and black to a very wide selection of colors, including opalescent and metallic tones. The amount of coloration absorbed will vary depending on the porosity of the gourd surface. Very often, a colored-wax finish will reveal interesting patterns in the shell that were not visible on the untreated surface. For interesting and unexpected results, use more than one shade of polish or wax.

Waxes and polishes can be reapplied periodically to the gourd surface to restore luster and sheen. Occasional light buffing is often all that is required to restore sheen. One word of caution: the color pigments contained in wax polishes are subject to fading when exposed to the sun. Some of the colors change hue slightly even after a period of time in indirect light. It's very important, therefore, to keep all such finished gourds out of direct sunlight.

One floor finish that is quite different from waxes and polishes is an acrylic polymer (available under the product name Future®, manufactured by the Johnson Company). It's easy to apply to a gourd and provides protection from water and normal indoor use.

OILS

Linseed oil, mineral oil, tung oil, and several furniture oils are also good choices. The oils penetrate the surface of the gourd and provide a rich luster, but they do not buff up to the sheen of a wax or a polish. Paint pigments, such as oil paints, can be mixed with linseed oil to provide a washed or transparent color effect. The tinted oil can be brushed, wiped, or rubbed onto the gourd surface, creating a soft surface with very delicate color tones. However, some oils, particularly tung oil, have a tendency to frost or become milky when they dry. Experiment on small gourds or gourd scraps before you apply an oil to your favorite project.

Leather softeners or oils designed to preserve and protect leather shoes and furniture can also be used to protect the gourd surface.

JEAN STO
Gourd's Night Ou
This gourd was shaded with shoe polish to achieve a subtle highlight of the neckline.

JOSEPH ULMER
Homage to Lucy

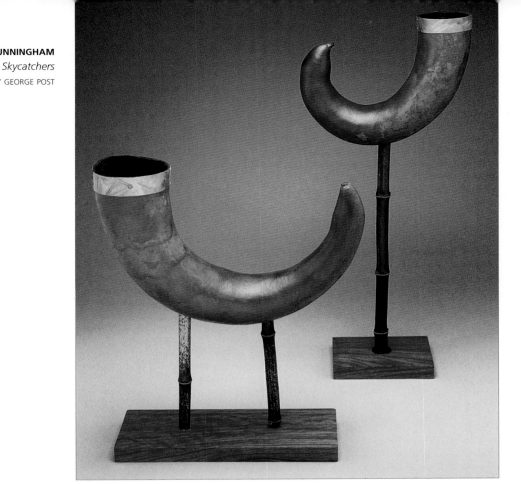

LIZ CUNNINGHAM
Skycatchers
PHOTO BY GEORGE POST

VARNISHES AND RELATED FINISHES

For a more durable finish, particularly when the gourd has already been painted with oils, acrylics, or watercolor paints, consider using a varnish or a synthetic resin product. What you choose will depend on personal preference, the recommendation of the manufacturer of the paints you have used, and the style of design used on the gourd.

Varnishes can be oil or water based and are available in a variety of finishes, including gloss, semigloss, satin, and matt. Some artists prefer a spray varnish that provides a very light protective film and allows much of the natural texture and surface of the gourd to predominate. Others prefer to paint the varnish directly on the surface. A very thick, protective, and glossy appearance can be produced by applying up to six coats of varnish. By carefully sanding between each coat, a shiny finish is created that not only protects the surface, but gives the gourd a dimension of luster quite distinct from the natural surface of the gourd shell.

There are many synthetic resin finishes sold in art and craft supply stores that are quite suitable for use on gourds. They are available both as sprays and in cans and come in several different surface finishes. Art stores also carry a variety of glazes and gels that can provide a very thick and textured protective coat.

Some of the varnishes and other finishes are advertised to have a UV inhibitor, which is supposed to inhibit the tendency of many

pigments, such as those in dyes and paints, to fade in the sunlight. Spar marine varnishes are specifically designed to reduce the effects of UV damage on boats. However, do not depend on this type of protection to guarantee colorfastness. In fact, these varnishes may yellow or otherwise alter the colors over which they are applied. Color media that are not colorfast, particularly stains, dyes, and inks, will probably fade in time, but perhaps not as rapidly when protected by a UV finish.

One factor to keep in mind when selecting a final protective coat is how that product will affect the color medium that has already been used on the gourd. Different varnishes, shellacs, and vinyl resins contain solvents or bases that will react with some color media (such as stains and dyes), causing them to run or bleed into each other. This is less a problem with oil-based and acrylic paints which are quite stable and inert once they are dry. Dyes, stains, inks, and watercolor paints are more likely to be affected.

Gourds that may be left outside should be treated with a wood preservative as well as a shellac or varnish. Weather can be harsh even on gourd surfaces that have been protected. Ideally, outside gourds should be kept in a covered area out of direct sunlight. In dampness and humidity, gourds can become mildewed, particularly if the interior is exposed through cracks or cuts in the gourd shell.

Interior Finishes

PAINTS, SPRAYS, AND STAINS

How you plan to use the finished gourd will help you choose an interior finish. For projects that will remain purely decorative, just scrape or sand the interior, clean out as much of the pulp as possible, and then tint, spray, or paint the inside. In coloring the interior of a gourd, you can use any type of paint, stain, or dye. Occasionally, thin stains and dyes may be absorbed by a particularly porous shell and may affect the exterior surface of the gourd. It's a good idea to test the finish on a small gourd or gourd scrap that is of similar shell density to the gourd you intend to use for your project.

Spraying with an air gun or aerosol paint can is the fastest way to paint or dye the irregular and porous interior surface. You can also daub on colors with a sponge or sponge brush, if the size of the opening allows access. If the gourd opening is too small to reach inside with a paint brush, simply pour the paint or dye into the gourd, swirl it around to cover all the surfaces, and then pour out the excess. A foam brush also works well for this purpose. Apply a very liberal coat of paint and allow it to soak in. Any type of paint is suitable: acrylic, tempera, even latex paint intended for the interior or exterior of houses can be used. Be sure to tape tissues or paper towels around the edge of the gourd to protect the outside from an errant dribble.

Textured paints are an interesting way to provide an appealing contrast or complement to the gourd surface. They frequently come with colors already mixed in (see page 68 in Chapter Three for examples of textured paint). Another related covering is flocking, a powdery coating that creates a velvety finish. Before applying the flocking, seal the interior, following the manufacturer's recommendations. Then, paint an enamel primer or special adhesive on the area to be flocked. While the area is still wet, you can either blow the flocking fibers onto the area or dust them on with a special applicator. When the adhesive is completely dry, lightly brush away the excess flocking; the remaining surface will be permanently covered with a soft texture.

PAM BARTON

PHOTO BY
SHERI SIEGEL

INTERIOR AS PART OF THE DESIGN

If you plan to use the interior surface as part of the design, you will first need to completely sand the inside to remove as much of the uneven porous layer as possible. Power wire brushes and sanders are very useful for this job. Once the interior is smooth, many decorative techniques can be used. Depending on the smoothness of the surface and the embellishment techniques you plan to use, the surface may or may not need a ground or base coat.

If you want to wood burn the interior, simply clean the surface as much as possible, and wood burn as you would on the exterior surface. If you wish to use paints, you will need to seal and prime the surface as you would any soft wood background. Some artists coat the interior of a bowl or platter with modeling clay to create a surface that can then be stained or painted. Other linings include handmade paper or paper mache, fabric or paper collage, or mosaics with beads or other found objects.

CREATING A WATERTIGHT GOURD

If you intend to use your gourd as a vase, a plant holder, or a container for nonedibles, there are several types of finishes you can use to make the gourd watertight.

PARAFFIN AND BEESWAX

One popular method is to use melted paraffin or beeswax to coat the porous interior. First thoroughly clean and smooth the gourd interior. Melt the paraffin or beeswax in a double boiler, taking great precaution not to spill any of the contents, since paraffin is highly flammable. While the paraffin is melting, heat the gourd in a warm oven (180°F or 82°C) for five minutes or until the gourd shell is completely heated through. It's important that the gourd is hot when you apply the paraffin so that the wax will penetrate the porous shell. If the gourd is cold, the wax will cool instantly on the surface and may turn white and flake off. However, be careful of the oven temperature; roasting a gourd in a hot oven may make it quite brittle.

The melted paraffin can then be applied with a brush, or for the most complete coverage, poured directly into the gourd interior. Wearing protective gloves, tip and roll the gourd so that the melted wax covers the entire inside surface. Pour out the excess wax or, to add additional weight and a flat surface to the base, allow the wax to harden in the base of the container.

If the wax has penetrated the gourd shell, or if it has dribbled on the exterior surface, it will affect the adhesion of any decorative finish. Therefore, as a final finish, you may want to wax the exterior, too.

A simple wood burned gourd from Peru is opened to reveal an elaborate crèche, complete with moveable figures.   COLLECTION OF PEGGY BAUMGARTNER

WOOD SEALERS, VARNISHES, AND POLYURETHANE FINISHES

For gourd containers that won't be used for holding food, you can also coat the interior with wood sealers, varnishes, or polyurethane finishes. Apply more than one coat so that the gourd shell will be completely sealed. Another finish to consider is plastic resin, a two-part product that when mixed together, can be applied to the gourd with a brush. It sets up rapidly, so you will need to work quickly once the mixture is made. Excess resin will drain to the bottom of the container and puddle. This can be an advantage if additional weight or stability is important. When dry, the resulting surface is shiny and very rigid and tends to make the gourd shell very solid.

PREPARING THE INTERIOR FOR USE WITH FOOD

Many people would like to use gourds for storing food but are worried about how to finish the interior in a safe way. For thousands of years, gourds have been used for eating utensils and as vessels for foods, either for storage, transportation, or cooking. Originally, the containers and utensils were simply thoroughly cleaned and then soaked for a period of time to remove the bitter taste. The length of time for soaking depended entirely on the gourd, since some shells have a particularly strong bitter taste.

Many cultures prescribed soaking the gourd in salt water; others specified fresh water. Some required that the utensil or container be boiled, while others simply advised soaking and renewing the water at intervals until the taste was not unpleasant. To create an interior safe for holding foods, you can follow this same procedure, too.

First, soak the gourd interior for up to several days in water to which you've added a tablespoon of baking soda. Pour out and renew the water at intervals, and take a small sip of the water to see if the bitter flavor is gone. If not, continue to soak the gourd.

Besides imparting a slight flavor, there is another concern in using gourds with food: Because of their porous nature, liquids have a tendency to penetrate the shell and to bead on the outside. In the past, the continuous evaporation process of the beaded water on the exterior surface kept the water inside the gourd canteen cool and refreshing. Today, however, when gourds are kept inside the house or on the table, this feature can present a problem. Consequently, most people prefer to seal gourds they plan to use to with food.

OILS

Products designed for sealing wooden cutting boards, salad bowls, and butcher block surfaces, available in most hardware and kitchen appliance stores, can also be used to create a food-safe gourd interior. Some kitchen oils, such as safflower or soybean oils, dry to form a hard surface film that is impervious to liquids. You will need to apply several coats of warm kitchen oil and allow each coat to thoroughly dry; the entire curing process will take about a month. This treatment can be repeated at intervals to renew the watertight film. These oils will not turn rancid and do not impart a flavor to foods. Although gourds treated with these products are safe to use with foods, their surfaces are still relatively soft and should not be cut upon with knives or used to hold hot foods. They can be washed with warm soapy water but should not be put in a dishwasher.

Another way to treat the interior of gourds intended for foods is with several coats of a 100 percent polyurethane finish. Make sure the interior surface is completely clean and smooth before you apply the finish. The first coat usually raises some of the porous material of the interior surface, so you will need to sand the surface carefully between each coat in order to have a smooth final finish. As with all other gourd dishes, these should be handled with care and washed by hand.

SUSAN CORREIA
The darkened interior of the gourd provides a dramatic frame for a piece of twisted seaweed.

EUGENIE GWATHNEY
This detailed scene is painted inside the gourd.

Stabilizing the Gourd

Many gourds grow with or are manipulated to have flattened bases to allow them to be stable and to stand upright. Unfortunately, most gourds wind up either with an uneven bottom surface or are later cut so that they don't balance, and it becomes necessary to provide a base to stabilize them. The way you have decorated the gourd will usually suggest a solution. Here are some options to consider.

DIANE WESTGATE
A stand made from copper tubing creates a striking accent.

MAKE A STAND

Use a separate ring to hold the gourd. Ready-made rings are available in many guises: wooden bracelets, curtain rod rings, napkin rings, woven wreaths, small baskets, clear plastic pipe cut to the appropriate height, and washers of a wide variety of materials and dimensions. You can stitch or glue these rings onto the bottom of the gourd or leave them unattached.

Create a gourd stand from gourd scraps. Cut out simple rings with or without legs and other design elements that complement the gourd decoration. Bevel the upper edge of the ring so that it fits the contour of the bottom of the gourd. Stain or paint the stand to match the gourd.

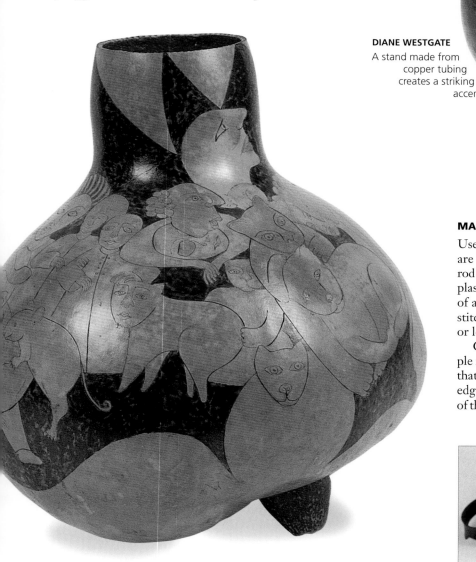

GRETCHEN CETERAS
You can use a piece of another gourd to make a balance or wedge to hold a gourd shell upright.

CREATE ADDITIONAL WEIGHT

Gourds can be stabilized with plaster of paris. Put rocks or pebbles inside the gourd. Mix the plaster of paris in a plastic bag and then cut off the corner so the plaster can drain into the gourd without spilling. The plaster will hold the added materials in place. Plaster of paris heats as it sets and must be allowed to dry for several days. As the plaster dries, moisture will leach out through the shell and will affect any surface embellishment you've added. It's best to pour in the plaster before you decorate the gourd.

Resin is another material that can be poured inside the gourd to form a watertight interior; the excess resin will puddle in the bottom of the gourd and provide additional weight. Like plaster of paris, resin heats while it is setting but does not create the same moisture problem, and most exterior embellishments will not be affected.

ADD ADDITIONAL MATERIAL:

You can stabilize a gourd by attaching something to the bottom to balance it. Many different objects and materials have been used successfully.

- A lump or ring of wood putty or modeling clay. This can be stained or painted to complement the gourd surface.

- A shell, stone, gourd fragment, or piece of wood. Glue the material in place with wood glue, or screw, stitch, or nail it in place.

- Tacks with decorative heads or small wooden plugs. These are readily available in hardware or craft stores.

- A material that complements or extends the material used in embellishment of the gourd. This may include vines, bark, or pinecones.

SAND THE BOTTOM

Sanding flat the bottom of the gourd is a good solution for stabilizing thick-shelled gourds where you don't run the risk of sanding through the shell. You must first determine the portions of the gourd bottom that need to be flattened. The easiest way to do this is to hold the gourd upright on a belt sander, if one is available. Otherwise, grind off the protruding bumps with a wood file or power sander. Be careful not to grind completely through the gourd shell or you will create a hole. To give the bottom a finished look, glue on a circle of felt or leather.

CUT OFF THE BOTTOM

If the gourd won't be used as a container, you can cut off a portion of the bottom to create a flat, even base. Set the gourd on a suitably sized container so that you can mark a line where you want to cut.

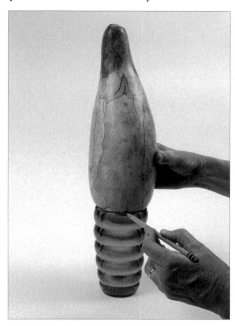

Use a craft knife to cut along the line. Clean out the loose pulp and seeds. Glue the gourd onto a piece of felt or leather to cover the hole and create a smooth base. Trim the edges of the material to conform to the shape of the gourd. You may want to glue a cord along the edge of the leather or felt to provide a finished look.

BEVERLY ROBBINS
You can make a doughnut of wood putty and press the gourd firmly on it so that it is held stable.

Inventive Ways to Stabilize the Gourd

SELMA BROWN
The polymer clay legs on this gourd are nicely integrated with the rest of the gourd design.

MIMI TURNER

DEBORAH MOSKOWITZ
The nest of dried seaweed is reflected in the textures and surface of the gourd, creating an integrated composition.

M. C. GLENN
A special basket woven and attached to this gourd holds it upright.
PHOTO BY ED WILSON

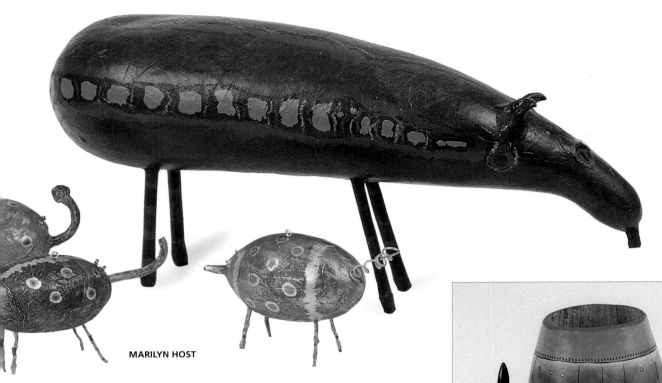

MARILYN HOST

LARRY PHILLIPS
A separate gourd piece was cut to reflect the turtle motif and to provide a dramatic stand for this bowl

SUSAN SWEET

Attaching Pieces to the Gourd

If your design requires attaching two or more gourd pieces to the main gourd, there are several ways to provide a secure and smooth join. Here are two simple projects that demonstrate the main methods. Don Weeke's project on page 135 demonstrates additional attachment techniques.

Candlestick

This holiday candlestick uses a reinforced join to attach two gourd pieces.

WHAT YOU NEED

2 gourd pieces with shells of similar thickness and density, cured and cleaned
File or sandpaper
Cheesecloth
White glue
Bowl of water

WHAT YOU DO

1. File or sand the two gourd pieces to insure a snug fit all along the join. Soak a strip of cheesecloth in a thick solution of white glue and water (Photo 1).

2. Wrap this strip along the back of the join, pressing firmly to make sure the join will be held secure (Photo 2).

3. Once the glue is dry, the join can be disguised in several ways. Here, we have glued on a small grapevine wreath with artificial berries. If the gourd shell is to be left natural, the join can be covered with another material that is glued or sewn in place, or it can be filled in with putty or wood filler, taking care to smooth the surface of the gourd.

Pitcher
with Handle

A channel join is used when a small gourd piece is added or attached to a larger gourd, such as was accomplished with this attractive pitcher.

WHAT YOU NEED

Bottle gourd, cured and cleaned
Dipper gourd, cured and cleaned
Pencil
Craft knife
Hand or power saw
Garden shears
File
Sandpaper
Hand or power carving tool
Wood glue
Masking tape
Wood filler or putty
Acrylic metallic copper paint
Paintbrush
Black shoe creme polish
Spray can of black acrylic paint

WHAT YOU DO

1. Mark the areas where you want to cut on both of the gourds (Photo 1).

2. With the craft knife, make slices along the marked lines to start the cut, then use a hand or power saw to cut off the pieces. Hold the handle alongside the pitcher to check the accuracy of your cut (Photo 2).

3. Trim the opposite end of the handle with the shears (Photo 3).

4. Use a file and sandpaper to clean all the cut edges and to trim the handle until it exactly fits the contour of the pitcher. Hold it against the pitcher and draw a line where the pieces are to be joined (Photo 4).

5. Make a groove along this line with the carving tool, making sure that the groove is wide enough to fit the handle. Be careful not to make a hole all the way through the gourd shell! (Photo 5).

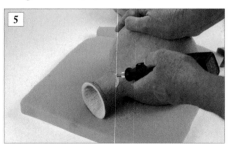

6. The groove provides a good bonding surface for the wood glue; apply a generous amount to the groove (Photo 6).

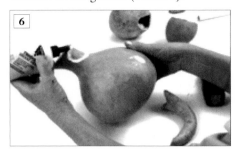

7. Press the handle into the channel and secure it with tape. Resist the temptation to test the bond because any slight movement may break the seal. Let the gourd handle dry overnight (Photo 7).

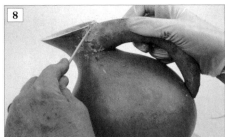

8. Fill in the join with wood filler or putty, taking care to sand all the edges smooth. Paint the pitcher with acrylic metallic copper paint. When dry, rub the entire surface with black shoe polish to create a darkened patina. Spray the inside with black acrylic paint (Photo 8).

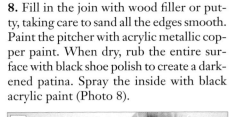

MARY WOJECK
By combining gourds and gourd pieces, the artist creates a wide variety of lifelike birds.
PHOTO BY EVAN BRACKEN

Animal Creations Using Joining Techniques

DICK LEWIS
This little gourd mouse was constructed by joining two ornamental gourds. The join is hidden behind a leather collar.

BILL KUPKA
These little koalas are built of several gourds and gourd pieces.
PHOTO BY BILL BUCKLES

MINNIE BLACK
This fanciful creature was created from many small gourds and gourd pieces, each artfully attached.

Handles, Lids, Hinges, and Hardware

The simplest way to carry a gourd is by the hole made in the shell. This example is from the Amazon region of Ecuador.

COLLECTION OF GINGER SUMMIT

HISTORICAL OVERVIEW

As gourd vessels were adapted to satisfy the needs of emerging societies, people developed many different strategies to increase the gourd's usefulness and effectiveness both for transportation and for storage. For example, gourds that were used to hold heavy items required handles to make them easier to carry and to provide a way for the gourds to be stored. Gourds often were hung in trees or on posts so that the contents were out of reach of rodents and other pests. Lids were improvised to protect the contents of the gourds from being spilled, contaminated, or otherwise damaged. Stands became necessary to stabilize the round gourd containers and protect the valuable contents from spilling.

The first and simplest handles were hand-size holes cut in the sides of the gourd container. Later, slings were devised of vines, cord, or strips of hide to allow people to carry and lift full and slippery gourds. Many examples of gourds that were wrapped in this manner are found in natural history museums. Handles of sticks were lashed to the edges of containers or poked through holes that were bored into either side of the gourd opening.

The very earliest lids were probably leaves or other natural objects draped over or stuffed into the openings of a gourd container. Openings plugged with corncobs, shells, stones, and carved wood can be found in many natural history museums in the United State and Europe. In Hawaii, storage containers were closed by inverting a large gourd over the opening in the bottom container; sometimes both the bottom and top gourds were then covered with a netting. This netting could be pulled up and tied over the cover gourd, securing the two halves together. Another technique involved covering both gourd sections with tightly woven basketry, which was then laced together to form a secure storage space.

This well-used water-scoop from Colombia consists of a stick handle that was lashed to a large gourd.

CASA ANTIGUA, REDWOOD CITY, CALIFORNIA.

HENRIETTA HAINES
The lids for these miniature containers are constructed of several beads that stack together.

CONTEMPORARY APPROACHES

Today's gourd artists use these same time-honored techniques. Modern interpretations are enhanced with gracefully carved openings and unusual new materials. Handles and lids can serve a functional purpose or be purely decorative. Either way, they provide a complement to the overall shape of the gourd.

Contemporary artists still make lids from corncobs, shells, vines or sticks, horns or antlers, rocks or beads. These materials are frequently attached with a cord to the body of the container so that they will not be misplaced. In addition to these methods, there are many other ways to create attractive and functional lids using new materials.

- A plug for a small hole can be devised out of almost any material. Corks and wood stoppers in a wide variety of diameters are available from hardware and housewares stores. Stoppers can be carved from wood or created from clay.

- The portion of the gourd that is cut from the opening is often used as a lid. If the opening has been cut with a fine-tooth saw, and if the cut is close to the vertical slope of the gourd, the lid can fit with a near-invisible joining. To accomplish the fit, be sure to sand the edges very lightly so that the fit remains snug. If the opening has been cut such that the piece does not fit securely, the top can be enlarged with a strip of leather glued to the edge. Or, you can use coiling (see examples on page 101) to create an extra rim that will slightly expand the diameter of the gourd opening and provide a tight fit. Both the edge of the container and the edge of the lid can be extended with a vertical firm rim to create a rigid closure.

DIANE ARMSTRONG
A branch was inserted into
a hole and glued in place near the top edge of this graceful pitcher.
Then it was lashed to the gourd at the base.
PHOTO BY ROLF MENDEZ

ETHEL OWEN
This contemporary
artist cut the gourd
itself to create a
handle.
PHOTO BY DALE LEWIS

DYAN PETERSON

PHOTO BY TIM BARNWELL

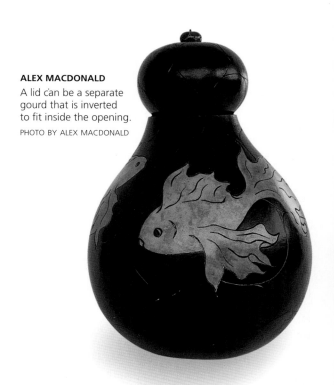

ALEX MACDONALD
A lid can be a separate gourd that is inverted to fit inside the opening.

PHOTO BY ALEX MACDONALD

NAN TOOTHMAN
The artist carefully cut the lid from the gourd so that the pieces fit snugly together. The shape of the cut complements the overall design.

PHOTO BY
KAREN A. BAGGOTT

EUGENIA GWATHNEY

CHRIS HOBACK
Sticks inserted through holes in the gourd shell utilize ancient techniques with very contemporary results.

MAYUMI TSUKUDA
Using a technique frequently found on handmade baskets, the artist lashed a handle to a gourd creating a strong and functional gourd basket.

PHOTO BY TOSHIHIRO NIIYAMA

AMI DIALLO
PHOTO BY ARTIST

Handles, Lids, Hinges, and Hardware **51**

HINGES

Lids frequently require a hinge of some type to attach the lid to the container so it will not become misplaced. If the container does not have a handle, a specific connection between the lid (or door) and the container must be created. Here are several options.

- Holes can be made in both the lid and the container and joined together with rings, loops of leather, or wire or cord.

- A strip of leather or other firm material can be nailed or otherwise secured to both the lid and the container, acting as a hinge.

- If the container is lined, the lining itself can provide a hinge between the lid and container.

- Several ready-made hinges that can be nailed, screwed, or riveted to both the lid and the container are available in hobby and hardware stores

DICK LEWIS
This hinge was created with a separate piece velvet lining.

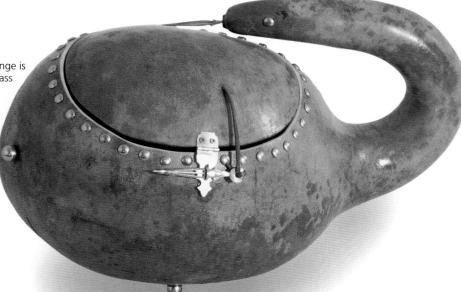

AMI DIALLO
A decorative brass hinge is complemented by brass upholstery tacks and small brass beads, one of which serves as a foot to stabilize this box.
PHOTO BY SUE SMITH

HARDWARE

Gourds can be used as the bodies for many different objects in the house, such as lamp bases and shades, clocks, or frames for pictures and mirrors. The hardware for such items is sold in most complete hobby and craft-supply stores. Select only the best thick-shelled gourds for these projects. Hardware for these purposes usually comes with screws or nails. When you use these fasteners on a gourd, be sure to reinforce them with strong glue. Rivets, or small bolts that are anchored in place with a washer on either side of the gourd shell, will provide extra strength to the attachment. If the gourd shell is thin or porous, carve a block of wood to conform to the inside curvature to anchor the screws or nails. If reinforced in these ways, the gourd can be treated as any other wooden object to decorate the house in unexpected and delightful ways.

DUANE TEETER
Clock fittings are attached to the interior of this gourd and the pendulum hangs through an opening at the narrow end of the clock face. A small gourd disc was decorated to complement the wood-burned designs on the face and provides the necessary weight for the pendulum.

M.C. GLENN
This lamp was made from two gourds. A small gourd rests securely on a rope base and is wired with lamp fittings. The gourd lamp shade has holes in the top to allow the warm air to rise.
PHOTO BY ED WILSON

In Portugal, an ingenious bank was fashioned out of a gourd. The money is put into a slot in the upstairs window. A rod is attached to the door and extends through the gourd to an opening in the back wall. A lock fits into the loop at the end of the rod. When the lock is removed, the door can be opened.

COLLECTION OF KAY HATTEN

Repairs

Gourds are woodlike spheres and must be handled with care. Like wood, gourd shells vary considerably in thickness, density, and brittleness. Age, moisture, and gourd type are factors that influence the strength of the shell.

HISTORICAL OVERVIEW

In most primitive cultures, gourds were very important items in the household and in other aspects of daily life. Small or undecorated gourd containers were frequently recycled when they broke. Shards or gourd fragments were used for other purposes, such as eating utensils, digging tools, and blades to scrape hides or smooth pottery. However, large gourds, especially those that were decorated, were very valuable both for their function and as symbols of wealth. Netting, basketry, and clay or pitch linings (applied both internally and externally) were used by many cultures around the world to protect their valuable gourd objects.

If and when cracks did occur, the gourd was often mended. Stitching gourds with crude or fine cord was done on every continent throughout the ages. Usually the stitches that were used were very simple and served to hold the pieces together rather than to decorate them. Examples of repaired gourds that were used for a wide variety of domestic purposes can be seen in museums around the world. In Africa, pitch combined with metal plugs was used, particularly on the bottom surfaces of large containers where abrasion wore through the gourd.

Usually there is no attempt to hide or disguise a repair. Collectors often find that a repair in a gourd attests to its usefulness and value to the owner; the repair adds charm to the item.

African gourds that have been elaborately carved are frequently repaired with lacing and pitch to extend the usefulness of this important household item. COLLECTION OF GINGER SUMMIT

CONTEMPORARY GLUING AND LACING

Today, many materials are available to repair cracks or splits so that the repairs are nearly invisible. Many wood glues and hobby adhesives will effectively repair a dry porous shell. Once a repair is made, it should be reinforced with tape or rubber bands until the adhesive is thoroughly dry and the pieces have bonded.

Contemporary gourd artists continue to lace cracks together, but lacing is also regarded as an embellishment.

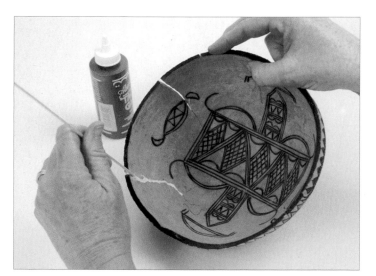

Tacky glue can be used to mend cracks in a gourd shell. Tape the gourd securely until the glue dries. This gourd is from Nigeria. COLLECTION OF KATHIE MCDONALD

REPLACING A STEM

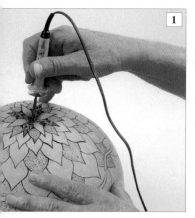

Frequently the gourd's stem will break off during the drying, cleaning, or crafting processes. Occasionally the stem on a particular gourd is not attractive or has a bend or shape that doesn't complement the design. It's a simple job to replace a stem with one you prefer, but the process must be done carefully, as described below.

1. If the end of the stem to be attached to the gourd is not smooth, cut it so that it has no jagged edges.

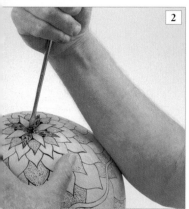

2. With a the leather awl or woodburning tool, make an initial hole in the spot where the stem was originally attached to the gourd (Photo 1).

3. Expand the hole by twisting a screwdriver in it or by drilling with an appropriate diameter drill bit (Photo 2).

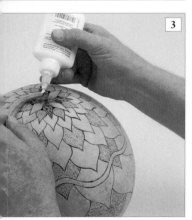

4. Glue the stem in place with a strong wood glue (Photo 3).

5. Once the glue is dry, scorch the join lightly with the wood-burning tool to create lines that will help the stem blend in with the gourd body (Photo 4).

This area can be daubed with furniture polish or a light stain to further conceal the join. Even when the glue is completely dry, the new stem should be handled with care. Although it will look natural, a glued-on stem is never as strong as the original.

DUANE TEETER

WORKING WITH A FLAW

Occasionally a gourd will have a flaw, such as an indentation, crack, or scar that is too large to be removed but can be coordinated to become an integral part of the design. Let the gourd itself suggest the appropriate design solution.

A gourd may have a perfect shape, size, and shell thickness but be marred by a crack or hole that interferes with a design you have selected. Several products on the market can repair these flaws with minimal visual effect. Make any repairs to the surface before starting any other surface treatment. Carefully filled in and sanded, a flaw can be made to disappear. Wood dough, a puttylike product manufactured by several companies and widely available in hardware stores, comes in several shades of tan and brown. Fill in the flaw with the wood dough and allow it to dry. Lightly sand the surface, and, if necessary, apply a light touch of furniture polish or stain to match the gourd's color. Some putties are specially formulated for use with stains or paints, while other products resist surface treatment. Read the label of the product before you use it.

You can make your own filler with a mixture of gourd sawdust, accumulated from sawing, sanding or carving a gourd shell, and white glue. This mixture is useful for filling any surface blemish or a crack; when sanded, it's almost invisible against the gourd surface mosaic. This is a particularly good repair material to use when the gourd is to be dyed or covered with a transparent coloring, because the mixture is often difficult to detect on a natural gourd shell.

MARY PRYOR
Warped but Happy

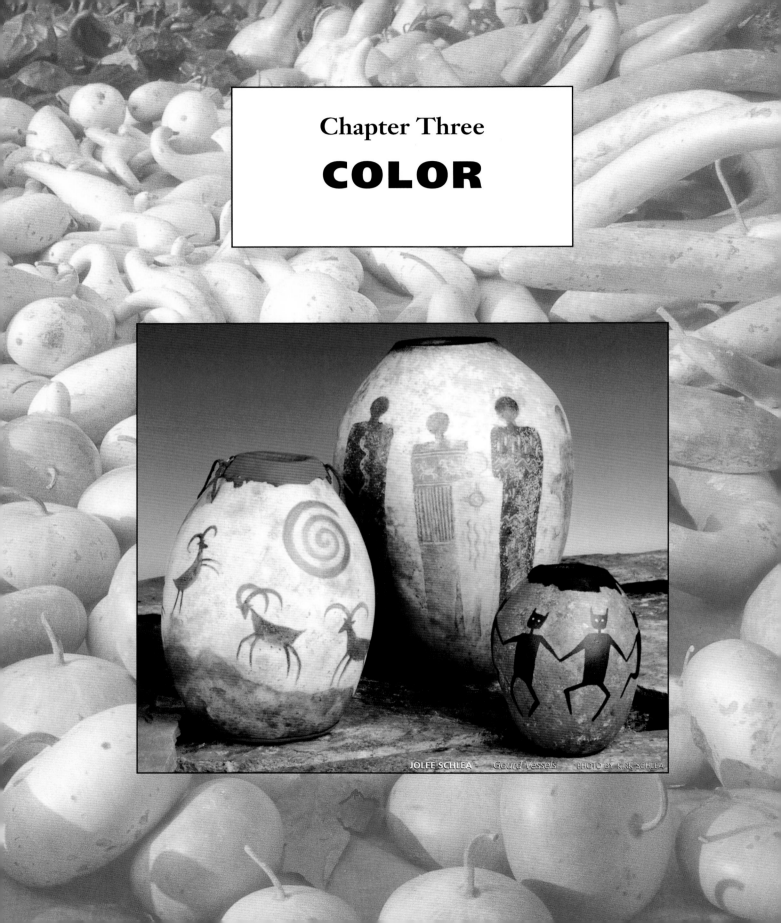

Chapter Three
COLOR

JOLEE SCHLEA *Gourd Vessels* PHOTO BY KIRK SCHLEA

HISTORICAL OVERVIEW

Bright colors were rarely used on early gourds. To achieve subtle coloration, the gourd was rubbed with natural stains or soaked in a dye bath. This use of dye is seen on very old gourds from Africa, South America, and Hawaii.

Gourds from Mexico predating the arrival of Europeans were covered with an extremely delicate and unusual style of color embellishment that is seldom used by contemporary artists. The gourds were first covered inside and out with a thick coat of lacquer. When this coat was dry, it was covered with a second coat of a different color. Once the second coat dried, portions were scratched away to reveal the color of the first coat. Intricate patterns were created in this manner. Today's artists from Mexico use bright enamel paints to embellish gourds. Usually the entire gourd is covered inside and out with a background base coat, and then elaborate designs of flowers, birds, or other natural motifs are painted on the exterior and the interior of the shell. Similar designs are used on maracas and other gourd instruments from Mexico and Central America.

North American Indians began to decorate their gourds with paints after the Europeans arrived and introduced these materials. Using tempera paints, Indian artists painted rattles and bowls with designs that complemented specific tribal ceremonies. Because gourd objects from this period were not protected with an overcoat, they suffer from flaked and peeling paint.

Today, art stores are stocked with a vast array of color media; new materials, tools, and techniques are constantly being introduced. Most color media intended for use on paper or wood is highly suitable for gourds as well. Your selection should be determined by the design and the effect you want to achieve, as well as by your own artistic preferences. It is also important to consider the final purpose of the decorated gourd, because color media vary in terms of color fastness, toxicity, and response to the gourd surface.

A multicolored Mexican lacquered gourd
COLLECTION OF CHRIS HOBACK

Mexican gourds are frequently painted with enamel paints in bright floral motifs.
COLLECTION OF NORMA A. FOX

Waxes and Polishes

You may want to create a very subtle color on the gourd surface—perhaps a darker (or lighter) shade that will enhance the natural mottled pattern of the gourd surface. Floor waxes, furniture and leather polishes, and shoe polish can produce this effect, enriching the surface mosaic while remaining very neutral or natural in appearance. (See the section on Exterior Finishes on page 33 for a more complete description.)

Keep in mind that after polishes or waxes have been applied to a gourd surface, it is not possible to use paints on that surface. The wax will act as a resist and prevent paints from absorbing into, or adhering to, the shell.

SPECIAL HAWAIIAN TECHNIQUE

A unique technique for dying gourds was developed in ancient Hawaii and was used through the early 18th century. Details of how this method was done are unconfirmed, and reports by Europeans who visited the islands have provided conflicting information. Currently, Dr. Bruce Ka'imiloa Chrisman in Hawaii is trying to revive not only the cultivation of gourds, but the ancient means of dying them as well.

The exact methods used to stain gourds with such precise pattern remain a mystery to this day.
KAUAI MUSEUM, LIHUI, KAUAI, HAWAII

According to his research, the procedure was as follows. As soon as a mature green gourd was cut from the vine, an intricate design was scratched into the epidermal "skin" layer. Over the next few weeks, the gourd's shell sealed beneath the epidermal injuries as the gourd healed. The gourd top was then opened, some of the seeds and pulp were removed, and the gourd was filled with a natural dye. The dye was left in the gourd to leach through the shell and stain the portion that was still covered with normal epidermis, and the sealed area prevented the dye from coloring the pattern that had been exposed by the scratch carving. After a period of time, the dye was poured out, the remaining epidermal skin was cleaned off, and the entire gourd was left to dry. Examples of this technique in museums in Hawaii and elsewhere attest to the superb workmanship of early artisans.

DR. BRUCE KA'IMILOA CHRISMAN
The artist recreated a traditional Hawaiian container by embellishing a gourd with stained geometric patterns and filling the opening with a seashell.

Inks, Stains, and Dyes

If you plan to color the gourd with stains or dyes and want the maximum penetration of color medium, don't apply a sealant to the gourd surface first. And although the gourd surface needs to be clean and smooth, don't sand it. Sandpaper will leave minute scratches that may encourage dyes to run, bleed, or otherwise invade unintended areas. The tiny scratches may also show up slightly darker when the gourd is stained or dyed and thereby detract from the gourd's natural coloration and absorption pattern. If any sanding is needed to remove dried epidermis, use a 0000 steel wool.

Contemporary carved gourds from Peru are frequently dipped in an aniline dye bath prior to carving.
COLLECTION OF LEN AND ANNA SHEMIN, BERKELEY, CALIFORNIA

INKS AND MARKING PENS

Artist inks and permanent marking pens are frequently used to decorate gourds because they are readily available in a wide range of colors and are so easy to use. You can find many different brands of inks and colored marking pens in good stationery and art supply stores. Depending on the brand, you can, to some degree, blend ink colors and lines by daubing the design with a cotton swab dipped in alcohol while the ink is still wet.

The greatest drawback to inks and ink marking pens is that colors are affected by sunlight. Even inks that are advertised as permanent are susceptible to fading. Black is the one ink that will maintain the same intensity over time. Marking pens made from oil-based paints are more colorfast than those made of ink. Oil-based marking pens come in many colors and are opaque, which gives them a very different effect than ink pens. These pens are excellent for providing highlights and fine detail to a design.

Children enjoy decorating gourds with colored marking pens, often using water-based pens. On small ornamental gourds that have relatively more porous shells, these pens create colorful designs with minimum mess.

It's a good idea to sketch your design on the gourd shell with a pencil and then fill in with permanent marking pen. Allow plenty of time for the ink to dry and then wipe the shell with a protective covering. In this case, the gourd was wiped with a white wood stain to provide a light glaze.

WOOD STAINS

Wood stains, found in most paint and hardware stores, are generally pigments or dyes dissolved in an oil base. They come in many shades and often can be mixed with additional tints, available in good paint stores, to create new hues or stains of greater intensity. Once applied to a gourd surface, they penetrate deeply into the shell and cannot be removed. To subtly enhance the natural patterns that mottle the gourd's surface, wood stains are frequently used on gourds that are not otherwise decorated.

GINGER SUMMIT
White wood stain was used to tint this gourd to go with the nylon cord that forms the handle and base.

Ink Transfer Pattern

If you are nervous about drawing your own design on a gourd shell, several products are available in art and craft supply stores that can help you transfer a pattern onto the shell. The product being used in this example is a Transfer Pen, available in fabric supply stores.

WHAT YOU NEED

Gourd, cured and cleaned
Power or hand cutting tool
Sandpaper
Transfer pen and paper
Scissors
Masking tape
Permanent marking pens
Floor wax and soft cloth

WHAT YOU DO

1. Cut an opening in the gourd and remove the pulp and seeds. Sand the cut edge smooth.

2. Trace the pattern using the paper and ink pen provided (Photo 1).

3. Cut out and tape the design you have traced, ink-side facing the gourd.

4. Rub the back side of the paper to gently transfer the ink pattern onto the gourd shell (Photo 2). Remove the paper, checking to make sure you have transferred all the design (Photo 3).

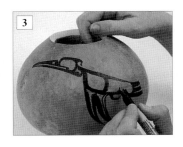

5. Fill in the outline with permanent marking pens (Photo 4). Polish the finished gourd with wax to bring out the natural texture of the shell. This design used scars on the gourd surface for the center of the flowers.

Be cautious when applying a finish to a gourd decorated with inks and marking pens. Shellac, varnish, lacquer, and polyurethane may cause many of the brands and colors to blend and run together, sometimes with disappointing results. Fixatives that can be sprayed very lightly over the gourd with very little impact on the design are available at art and craft supply stores.

Wood stains also are frequently used in combination with engraving or carving techniques. You will achieve very different results if you stain the gourd before it is carved, rather than after it is carved. For an interesting look, try combining the two techniques; stain some areas of the shell before carving and some after carving (see page 91).

LEATHER DYES

Leather dyes are frequently used on gourds because their beautiful and rich colors penetrate the gourd surface and enhance the texture and the mottled patterns of the natural shell. Dyes designed for fabric don't work very well on gourds.

Leather dyes are easy to use and can be purchased at leather supply outlets, craft stores, and shoe repair shops. They are available in several brands, which differ according to the type of solvent used to carry the colorant. Most brands are alcohol based; some are dissolved in mineral spirits. Leather dyes can be applied to the gourd with a foam brush, a dauber, or a brush. They come in a wide range of colors. To create even more shades, the dyes can be mixed with one another, either in a separate container or directly on the gourd.

These dyes absorb completely into the shell and provide rich but transparent hues that allow the natural surface mosaic of the gourd shell to show through. The soft, natural looking texture can then be waxed or varnished.

KRIS THOENI

PEGGY BAUMGARTNER
Dyes and stains were allowed to drip on this gourd to create interesting patterns.

CONSIDERATIONS WHEN USING LEATHER DYES

There are, however, some drawbacks to working with these dyes.

• Because they are very thin or fluid, it's often difficult to control the dye on the smooth rounded gourd surface, and the dyes easily mix or blend with neighboring colors. After the dye penetrates the gourd surface, it is difficult to remove a mistake. This can be a serious problem if the gourd has been sanded or scraped, and microscopic channels cause the dyes to bleed.

• In direct sunlight, dyes tend to fade to varying degrees. Even in indirect light, some colors are unstable and will, over time, diminish in intensity or change hue. By protecting the dyed surfaces with a UV-inhibiting varnish, it is possible to delay or substantially reduce the impact of sunlight, but some color alteration is likely.

• No universal standards have been developed for the color nomenclature of dyes. Labels for colors are not consistent between brands. In fact, even within a single brand, colors may vary considerably between lots. Moreover, reactions of dyes to different gourd shells may produce slightly different color hues. This can be seen when several gourds are dyed with a single bottle of dye at the same time. Consequently, hue, shade, and color intensity are variables that are often not only unpredictable but difficult to control.

Leather dyes can be used to cover the gourd shell completely or to fill in portions of the design. When covering large areas of the gourd, use a sponge brush to insure even coverage. Allow the dye to soak into the shell, particularly if you are covering the porous interior. Once the dye is dry, wipe off the excess with a damp sponge or towel. The beautiful tinted surface can be protected with wax, varnish or any other polish you prefer.

Leather dyes can also be used much like paints to color in portions of a design or pattern. Most artists woodburn the outlines into the gourd shell first; the grooves made by the wood burner help to prevent the dyes from running or bleeding into each other.

MARILYN HOST

SAFETY GUIDELINES

When working with dyes, many safety precautions are important.

- Always wear rubber gloves. Dyes that are dissolved in solvents are often very toxic and should not come in contact with the skin. Fabric dyes in powder form are also toxic and should be handled with care.

- Always work in a well-ventilated work space. A mask is a good idea, although inexpensive masks available in hardware stores are designed for protection against dust particles, not vapor fumes. This type of mask is very important to wear when mixing dye powders. The vapors of the dye solvents are also toxic, and prolonged exposure to the fumes should be avoided. Look for masks that protect against vapors and fumes if you want to avoid any exposure.

- Be aware of fire danger. Store all dyes and applicators in accordance with the instructions on the labels provided by the manufacturer.

Airbrushes and Stencils

AIRBRUSHES

The airbrush is a flexible tool that can be used with many different kinds of paints, stains, and dyes. Airbrushes come in a wide variety of styles, but there are generally three main components: 1) a pressure air supply, 2) a container or jar for the color medium, and 3) a nozzle with controls for the flow of air and color.

The source of the air supply is the feature of greatest variability. One model is equipped with an aerosol can of compressed air that can usually be attached directly to the nozzle; the nozzle in turn is connected to a jar of paint or even to a marking pen. Other models come with a small air compressor connected to the nozzle with a hose. The more elaborate the equipment, the greater the control the artist has over both the flow of the air and the spread of the color.

Many effects can be created with an airbrush. Often it is used to create gradual shading to highlight portions of the gourd, such as around the neck or around the bottom of the gourd, or as a transition between highlights of design or embellishment. Usually the manufacturer of the airbrush system will provide instructions on the use of the tool and will suggest techniques for its use.

DONNA SOSZYNSKI
Leaves were used as silhouettes and patterns for stencils. The airbrush blends the colors to create the effect of autumn leaves.

Bird Stencil with Marking Pens

A simple-to-use system combines an aerosol spray can of propellent with a marking pen. The advantage of this system is the ease of changing both the colors and the type of line. The primary disadvantage is that the can of propellent does not last long!

WHAT YOU NEED

Round gourd, cured and
  cleaned
Power or hand cutting tool
Line drawing
Stencil paper
Craft knife
Spray adhesive
Can of aerosol spray
  propellent
Marking pen
Length of upholstery
  braiding
Strand of beads
White glue
Floor wax and soft cloth
Round, black curtain ring
  for stand

WHAT YOU DO

1. Cut an opening in the gourd and clean out the pulp and seeds.

2. Place the stencil paper over the design you want to use. Cut out the design by tracing over it with the craft knife (Photo 1).

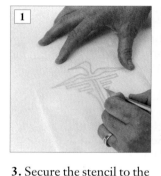

3. Secure the stencil to the gourd with spray adhesive, making pleats as necessary to conform to the curvature of the gourd. Attach the spray can to the marking pen and spray the ink onto the gourd surface that is exposed by the stencil (Photo 2).

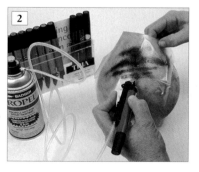

4. When the paint is dry, remove the stencil (Photo 3).

5. Around the opening of the gourd, glue on a length of braiding and, beneath it, the strand of beads. Finish the gourd by wiping on a coat of the floor wax. Sit the gourd on a round stand to stabilize it.

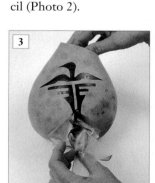

STENCILS

Stencils and silhouette forms can be used on gourds in a variety of ways and with many different media. Stencils can be used with airbrushes to silhouette or outline forms that are repeated randomly or in a regular sequence. Stencils are also frequently used with acrylic paints. They can be temporarily secured to a gourd with spray adhesive and then filled in with a paintbrush or a sponge. Ready-cut stencils are available in a wide variety of sizes and patterns. You can also purchase clear acetate sheets and make your own stencil patterns with a craft knife or fine-tip wood burner. Because stencils are usually intended for use on a flat surface, you will probably need to cut and "pleat" them to the contours of the gourd. Use clear tape to completely cover any cuts you make in a stencil where you do not want paint to penetrate.

Another useful material when using an airbrush, stains, or paints is a masking fluid that blocks out selected spaces of the gourd shell that you don't want to paint or color. Paint the masking fluid onto the portion of the shell you want to remain clear and allow it to dry. Apply paints or colors around and over the masking fluid. After the colored paints are dry, peel off the masking fluid; the space it was covering will be completely clear.

The following two projects use different airbrush methods.

Gourd with Antler

WHAT YOU NEED

Round gourd, cured and
    cleaned
Power or hand cutting tool
Line drawing
Stencil paper
Craft knife
Spray adhesive
Airbrush system with jar
    of paint, stain, or dye
Antler that fits curve in
    gourd body
Handful of Spanish moss
Scrap of rawhide
White glue
Tapestry needle
Artificial sinew

WHAT YOU DO

1. Cut an opening in the gourd and clean out the pulp and seeds.

2. Place the stencil paper over the design you want to use. Cut out the design by tracing over it with the craft knife (Photo 1) and secure it to the gourd with spray adhesive.

3. Hold the airbrush 4 to 6 inches (10.2-15.2 cm) from the gourd and spray in the design (Photo 2). You may also use the pieces you have cut out of the stencil to spray silhou-

ettes on the gourd shell. After you have sprayed all of the designs on the gourd, use the airbrush to shade in the neck and base of the gourd as well.

4. Glue the rawhide around the gourd opening. With the tapestry needle, poke two adjacent holes through the gourd near the opening and two others toward the base. Place the antler vertically between these holes and use the sinew to lash it to the gourd. Tuck the moss under the antler to continue the theme of browsing deer.

Paints

Many gourd artists take advantage of the wide variety of paints available today in order to turn gourds into beautiful works of art. Depending on the paint you select, you can achieve many different effects.

The opacity of the paint you use will determine how you will need to prepare the exterior surface. Watercolors, for example, are transparent and are absorbed best on an untreated gourd shell. Acrylic or oil paints that have been thinned to the point of transparency work best when painted over a light coat of varnish thinned with mineral spirits.

Some artists treat the gourd like a shaped canvas, using opaque acrylic or oil paints to cover the surface completely with figures and faces, objects or scenes. For this style of painting, prepare the gourd surface as you would a canvas. The selection of sealer and base coat will be partially determined by the final paints to be used. Follow the recommendations of the paint manufacturer for the appropriate base coat.

Sometimes you may want to cover only part of the gourd surface with opaque paint and leave the remaining shell natural. To do so—before you paint the design—seal the entire gourd surface with a thinned coat of shellac (thinned with alcohol) or varnish (thinned with mineral spirits).

NANCY LEE SCHLENDER
Colorful Geometrics

OILS AND ACRYLICS

The primary distinction between types of paints is the binding material that supports the color pigments: vegetable oils in the case of oil paints, natural emulsions in tempera paints, waxes in pastels, and synthetic resins in acrylics. Each type of paint has individual requirements as far as how the ground, or gourd, should be prepared, how the paint can be applied, and how it can be manipulated to create greater or lesser transparency, texture, color blending, etc. Both oil and acrylic paints can be thinned down to create almost a wash effect, or can be applied very thick to build up interesting surface textures. Both types of paints are available with enormous color choices that can be blended by the skillful artist so that the design is not limited by manufacturer options.

Oils and acrylic paints are the most reliable media for colorfastness and permanence. Acrylics can be combined with additional gels and media to build up a wide variety of textures and finishes. A well-stocked artist supply store offers many products intended for paper or canvas that can be used to paint gourds.

All paints should be sealed once they are dry; the choices range from one light spray to several coats of shellac, varnish, or polyurethane, depending on the type of paint and the final surface finish that is desired. Follow the recommendation of the paint manufacturer for the sealer that is best for the materials you have used.

LINDA EGLESTON

JEANETTE ROL
Qua

JANEICE SCOFIELD
Desert Lizards

KAREN MARTIN

Piggy Bank

This delightful piggy bank uses a simple but attractive painting technique that covers the entire surface, and features the two attachment methods illustrated on pages 44-46.

WHAT YOU NEED

Small round gourd, cured and cleaned
Several small gourd pieces, cured and cleaned
Power or hand cutting tool
File or sandpaper
Cheesecloth
White glue
Bowl of water
Pencil
Craft knife
Hand or power saw
File
Sandpaper
Hand or power carving tool
Wood glue
Masking tape
Wood filler or putty
Acrylic marbleizing paint kit
Clear varnish
Paintbrush

WHAT YOU DO

1. Cut off the end of the gourd to create an opening that will become the pig's nose. Clean out the pulp and seeds.

2. Cut four gourd pieces of similar height and diameter to use for the pig's legs. A good source for these is the neck of a dipper gourd. Attach the four legs using the channel technique described on pages 45 and 46.

3. Cut ears from the ends of other gourds, and attach them to the body using the channel method described on pages 45 and 46, Photos 1, 2, and 3.

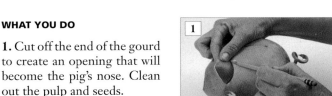

4. Fill in the join with wood putty. When the putty is dry, sand the join smooth (Photo 4).

5. Using a kit designed for marbleizing, first cover the body with one or two coats of base paint (Photo 5).

6. After the base coat is completely dry, pour a small amount of one darker and one lighter color onto a smooth surface. Dip the sponge in the paint and daub the paint onto the surface of the pig. Use the dark color first and then repeat the process with the light color (Photo 6).

7. Once the paint is completely dry, protect it with one or more coats of varnish.

Partially Painted Surface

If you want to cover only a portion of the gourd surface, you can achieve very attractive results by filling in a stencil pattern with a sponge and acrylic paint. Simply attach the stencil securely to the gourd with spray adhesive and sponge one of the colors around the edge of the stencil.

Fill in the design with complementary shades. After the paint is dry, remove the stencil. This project was completed with the addition of a leather hinge (see page 52 for examples of hinges), a bead and leather thong fastener, and a malachite stone glued in place for a handle.

Another simple painting technique is to stamp acrylic paint onto a gourd using a leaf or other natural object.

SUSAN SWEET

TEMPERA PAINTS

Tempera paints are a favorite of many crafts people, both for their availability and ease of use. The colors tend to be very bright and opaque and are generally lightfast. Follow the manufacturer's recommendation as to what kind of base coat to use before applying the tempera paints. Because tempera paints have an emulsion binder, they tend to dry with a slight film. They should still be protected with a light coat of varnish to protect them from handling.

PASTELS

Pastels are concentrated color pigments that have been pressed into a stick form with a binding medium. The binder for most pastel chalks is wax or gum; oil crayons and oil pastels are small sticks of pigment that have been oil impregnated.

There are many brands of pastel crayons on the market today. The less expensive brands tend to be more susceptible to fading in direct sunlight; reputable brands are more likely to be colorfast. All pastels should be protected with a light coat of varnish. A special type of fixative is necessary to protect oil pastels. You can use pastels on gourds much as you would on paper: colors can be built up to a certain thickness, then scraped, smoothed, and blended. In fact, pastels can be manipulated with much greater ease than paints or dyes. After applying the pastels to the gourd, rub the colored area with a cardboard point, a cotton swab, or your finger; you can also go over the area with a brush dipped in water or alcohol or—if you are using oil pastels—mineral spirits. The color effects are transparent, but the intensity of the color can be built up with additional layers of color. One of the pleasures of working with oil pastels is that colors can be added to or adjusted over a period of time.

LAVELL EVANS
Initiation

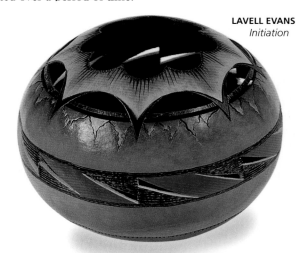

Oil-Pastel Easter Basket

For this pretty holiday basket you will need a gourd that rests securely on its side.

WHAT YOU NEED

Gourd, cured and cleaned
4 to 6 ornamental gourds, cured and washed
Pencil
Wood-burning tool
Power or hand cutting tool
Sandpaper
Oil pastels
Cotton swabs or cardboard point
Paintbrush
Linseed oil or mineral spirits (optional)
Protective finish designed for oil pastels
Polyurethane finish
Leather dyes in colors of your choice
Pearlescent acrylic paint

WHAT YOU DO

1. With the gourd on its side, sketch several large flowers onto the shell close to the vertical top of the gourd. Lightly wood burn the outline of all the flowers. Use a hand or power cutting tool to open the gourd by cutting along the outline of the uppermost petals. Remove the pulp and seeds and sand the interior and the cut edges.

2. Use the pastels just as you would crayons or chalk and color in the flowers (Photo 1).

3. With a cotton swab, add another color to create shading on the petals (Photo 2).

4. Rub the flowers with a cotton swab or a cardboard point to blend the colors, build up texture, and create soft shading (Photo 3). You can also use linseed oil or mineral spirits on a brush to blend and spread the colors.

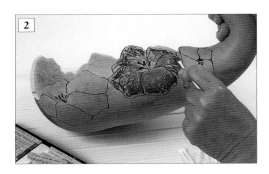

5. When the design is to your liking, seal the flowers with a protective finish especially formulated for oil pastels. Seal the inside of the basket with several coats of polyurethane finish. (A butterfly carved from an ornamental gourd and painted with acrylics is perched on the stem.)

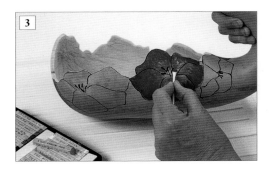

6. Paint the ornamental gourds with leather dyes. When dry, glaze them with a thinned coat of pearlescent acrylic paint.

TEXTURED PAINTS

There are many different products in art supply stores to-day that can add different textures to the gourd surface. Some of these products have color as part of the medium, making the addition of texture and color a one-step process. Other products are made of a paste or gel that can be applied to the gourd first and then painted or stained to match the rest of the design. Some gels can be mixed with a pigment or paint, such as acrylic, to achieve the desired tinting or hue, and then applied to the gourd.

Whatever the choice, the results can be fascinating: the gourd shape is maintained, but the texture and surface are quite altered. It's frequently difficult to identify that the base of the project is indeed a gourd.

Texture can be applied to the entire gourd or to selected portions of the design or pattern. These paints are a good way to cover blemishes or marks on the surface of a nicely shaped gourd, or to cover a repair that cannot be hidden with another style of embellishment.

ELAINE LONG
Buffalo Herd
This gourd was textured and the neck was coiled with pine needles.

LISA LARRIBA
Bear Pot
The center discs were painted and then protected as the rest of the gourd surface was covered with a textured paint. The bear lid is molded of clay.

ROWENA PHILBECK

Textured Container with Feathers

WHAT YOU NEED

Round gourd, cured and cleaned
Power or hand cutting tool
Steel wool or sandpaper
Stiff paintbrush
Granite-colored textured paint
White glue
Length of gray seam binding braid
12 to 15 gray feathers of similar size
1 large accent feather
2 to 3 gray beads

WHAT YOU DO

1. Cut an opening in the gourd and remove the pulp and seed. Before applying the textured paint, sand the shell to provide a good surface to which the paint can bond. Paint the surface with thick textured paint (Photo 1). You may need two coats to get an even coverage of the entire shell.

2. To provide a texture contrast to the granite paint, glue the feathers around the neck of the gourd (Photo 2).

3. Cover the ends of the feathers by gluing on the seam binding (Photo 3). To hide the ends of the binding, glue on an accent feather and several beads.

You can also spray on textured paint, a simple but somewhat messy method: The paint splatters over a great distance, so protect your work area with a backdrop. Roughen the gourd shell lightly with steel wool or sandpaper. Hold the gourd approximately 10 inches (25.4 cm) away from the can and spray evenly to completely cover the shell

(Above). Sometimes two coats are necessary to provide even coverage. Embellish the gourd to complement the new texture. In the example, a scrap of white leather was soaked in warm water and then molded to conform to the neck opening. Turquoise beads were stitched over the leather to secure it in place and to add a highlight to the otherwise white gourd.

RUTH EHRENKRANTZ
This gourd was covered with gold shoe polish to tint the surface and provide an overall shimmer to the shell.

Metallic Finishes

Art supply stores offer many different products that can create shiny, iridescent, or metallic finishes on gourd surfaces. These include polishes and waxes, metallic pens, paints, and powders, transparent washes, and metallic leaf. The choice of product is determined by the overall design of the gourd and the effect you want to create.

Metallic powders, designed for antiquing items or for providing a burnished effect, can be dusted on or rubbed into the painted surface of a gourd before applying a final coat of varnish. The metallic sheen will tend to collect in the depressions on the gourd surface. This is particularly effective in carved or engraved patterns.

Metallic finishes are also available in some shoe polishes and provide a shiny luster that enhances the base colors of the gourd. Select the polish that complements the color of the design, so that the overall effect is one of highlights.

Marking pens come in many different metallic colors, including gold, silver, bronze, and copper. The width of the tip ranges from fine to broad. Because these pens are paints rather than inks, the marks they produce are opaque. These pens are suitable for writing, drawing, and other fine-line detail.

Metallic paints can be applied with a brush, sponge, or dauber. Most of these products are an acrylic emulsion base in which the hues are created by metallic pigments. The color tends to be opaque, but many brands can be thinned with water to make them more transparent. These products can be used to fill in designs or to cover an entire gourd. The paint should be coated with varnish to keep the metallic from oxidizing and loosing luster.

DONNA SOSZYNSKI
Metallic paints can be airbrushed to suggest iridescent flames.

CHRIS HOBACK
Some acrylics come with glitter already mixed in the paints.

LORRAINE OLLER
Gold metallic pens create interesting designs on a stained gourd surface.

Some acrylic paints come with glitter or other shiny particles mixed into the paint. You can achieve a similar effect by sprinkling glitter on wet paint.

Metallic paints that are intended for automobiles (to hide scratches) or for model builders are another range of products to consider. These are usually enamel and are available in hobby or automotive supply stores in either spray can or bottle. The effect will be somewhat different than indicated on the container because these products are formulated to be applied to metal or plastic. However, they are available in a wide range of colors and produce interesting effects on a gourd surface. Drying time will vary according to the product.

A number of paint products are designed to create a pearlescent sheen and generally remain very transparent on a gourd shell. They go by the name of fluorescent, pearlescent, or interference, and work by absorbing and reflecting light rays in such a way that the overall effect varies by the orientation of the light and the position of the viewer. These paints can be applied to a gourd with a brush, dauber, or sponge to create accents in a design or to achieve an overall opalescent appearance. Iridescent paints are available in many very subtle color hues and are usually transparent but may be enhanced by applying several layers.

R.K. HEJNY
A rubbing of metallic powder provides a rich luster to a plain gourd shell.

PHOTO BY DREW DONOVAN

Gold Leaf Candle Holder

Metallic leaf or foil can create an extremely effective and dramatic finish for gourds. Other finishes may dull with age or fade in direct sunlight, but metallic leaf is permanently brilliant. These products involve several steps, as demonstrated in the following project.

WHAT YOU NEED

Small round
    gourd, cured
    and cleaned
Power or hand
    cutting tool
Paintbrushes
Special adhesive
Package of gold
    leaf or foil
Piece of
    cheesecloth
Metallic finish
Varnish
Length of thin
    gold braid
Craft glue
Brass candle cup

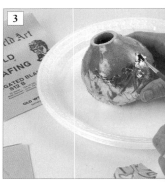

WHAT YOU DO

1. Cut an opening in the gourd and remove the pulp and seeds.

2. Paint the gourd surface with the special adhesive and allow it to dry for at least one hour (Photo 1).

3. Tear off very small pieces of gold foil and press them one at a time onto the gourd, overlapping the pieces so that the entire surface is covered (Photo 2).

4. Use a small, dry paintbrush to tamp down the edges (Photo 3).

SUSAN CANTWELL-HERNANDEZ

5. When you have covered the gourd surface with foil, rub it gently with the cheesecloth to make sure the metallic foil is in contact with the adhesive (Photo 4). Allow the adhesive to dry (about one hour) and then gently massage the foil with your thumbs and palms to make sure the pieces are blended and to flake off any excess. (Manufacturers of leaf or foil have many special finishes you can apply to create different effects or patinas on the finished project; none was used here.)

6. Coat the candle holder with varnish to protect the leaf. When dry, glue on a length of thin gold braid. The group of candle holders pictured above demonstrates the variety of metallic finishes that can be applied to a gourd.

RIDGE KUNZEL AND ROY SCHICK
Gold Leaf Kokopeli
Gold foil was applied to specific areas in the design.
COLLECTION OF HELEN BOS

SANDY WEBSTER
This evening bag is made from the bulb of a Maranka gourd, decorated with gold foil, beads, and thread.
PHOTO BY RUTH HARRIS

Gallery of Painted Gourds

JERRALDINE MASTEN HANSEN   PHOTO BY GREGG WUTKE

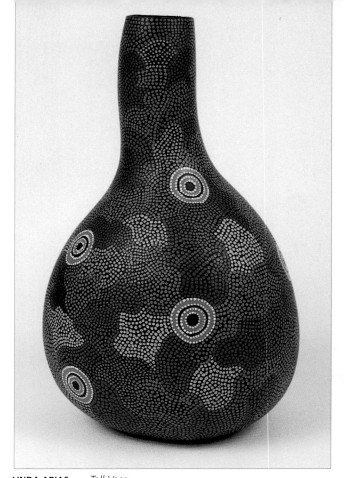

LINDA ARIAS   *Tall Vase*

JANICE BOLANDER

S. D. YOUNGWOLF

Chapter Four

PYROGRAPHY
AND
CARVING

ALEX MACDONALD

By blowing on a eucalyptus charcoal, this Peruvian artisan was able to produce delicate shading and detail.
COLLECTION OF LEN AND ANNA SHEMIN, BERKELEY, CALIFORNIA

Pyrography

HISTORICAL OVERVIEW

In ancient Africa, pyrography or pyro-engraving—the art of creating designs using heated tools or a fine flame—was commonly used to decorate gourds. This technique has been used to a much lesser extent in other cultures around the world. Beautiful pyro-engraved gourds found in Suriname on the northern coast of South America are actually the work of Africans who were brought to work in the plantations in the 18th century and fled into the jungles to form new communities. Today, local artists continue to embellish gourds in the traditional manner for special events, ceremonial occasions, and for the lucrative tourist trade.

Different pyrography techniques evolved in the many tribes and locations throughout Africa; designs on gourd bowls and containers reflect the traditional decorative patterns of each culture, as well as the skill of the individual crafts person. Styles of embellishment ranged from straight line geometric patterns or flowing bands to ornate figures and scenes encircling the entire surface of the gourd.

Traditions varied among tribes prescribing who could grow and embellish gourds, although in most cultures this was primarily the responsibility of women. In many of the tribes throughout Western Africa, women assumed all responsibility for cultivating, cleaning, and embellishing gourds. Gourds were not only a status symbol of a woman's household wealth, but a main feature of her dowry. In East Africa as well, women were in charge of cultivating and caring for gourds, but they were decorated and used by other members of the tribes.

The tools and techniques of pyrography were very simple: metal points and blades were heated in the fire and used to incise or scorch the surface of the shell. Often the flat surface of the burning tool was held against the surface of the gourd to scorch an area. To create fine decorative lines, the edge or tip of the tool was pressed or scraped against the shell.

In Peru, a different form of pyrography was used to shade in designs that had already been carved or engraved on a gourd shell. Gourds first were completely carved, and then individual figures were shaded by using the heat from a glowing eucalyptus or quinal stick. The stick was held close to the gourd and blown on to increase the intensity of the heat. By moving the burning element slowly or rapidly across the gourd surface, tones and shading could be created, ranging from light tan to reddish brown to almost black.

The intricate design on this lime container from New Guinea was burned on the gourd by blowing on the glowing tip of a sago palm frond.
COLLECTION OF ETHNIC ARTS, BERKELEY, CALIFORNIA

This collection of bowls from Nigeria was pyro-engraved using a spear-like metal point heated in a fire.
COLLECTION OF KATHIE MCDONALD

Acid burning was used to color the fish on this bowl from Peru.
COLLECTION OF LEN AND ANNA SHEMIN

Another technique perfected by the Peruvians required the application of several acids which, when dried close to a heat source, burned different shades into the gourd surface. A dilute solution of sulfuric acid was painted on the shell to create dark lines and small darkened design areas. Hydrochloric or muriatic acid was used to fill in for lighter tones. After the acids were brushed onto the surface, the gourd shell was then held over a heat source, such as an open fire, to dry the acids, which in turn burned the shell, creating a permanent and fade-proof decoration. Additions or corrections to the acid burned design were made by repeating these steps until the design was completed. A final and thorough washing with soap and water cleaned the residual acids from the gourd, and a polish of wax or oil restored a light sheen to the burned natural shell.

Note: *This is a very dangerous technique and should only be attempted by experienced crafters who can protect themselves from acid burns and toxic fumes.*

TOOLS AND TECHNIQUES

Pyrography is a favored technique of contemporary gourd artists. You can use a simple wood-burning tool with a general-purpose tip (available at most hardware stores and craft or hobby supply stores). Additional tips are very useful; some are themselves small designs, such as dots, circles, squares, diamonds, or teardrops, and can be combined in a number of ways to create interesting patterns.

Another type of wood-burning tool has been developed for the professional crafts person. It has an electronic power controller with a dial that regulates the amount of heat delivered to the tip, and interchangeable handpieces with a wide selection of tips. This tool delivers a hotter and more consistent burn than a hobby wood burner. Also, the variety of tips offer greater design options. (See Supply Sources on page 142.)

When pyro-engraving a hardshell gourd, it's important to be aware of variations in shell density; it can vary considerably among different types of gourds, gourds of different ages, individual gourds from the same vine, and even from area to area on a single gourd shell. Although it's unlikely you will burn through a hardshell gourd, density variations can affect the way the gourd surface interacts with the wood burner.

Another factor is the irregularity in heat delivered at the tip of a conventional wood burner. Heat dissipation occurs as the pen is drawn along a continuous line; the tip cools slightly from initial contact with the shell to the final lift point. From experience, you will develop a sensitivity to the interaction between the tip of the tool and the gourd surface. If you use your little finger to balance your hand as you burn the surface, you will be able to adjust the pressure on the tool and compensate for irregularities in surface texture. By experimenting and practicing on a variety of gourds, you will eventually be able to achieve a wide range of effects.

DEBBIE NORTON

RUTH EHRENKRANTZ

CHERYLN BENNETT   PHOTO BY SONNIA GORE

DESIGNING WITH THE WOOD BURNER

Drawing or designing with a wood burner is permanent: once the line is burned into the gourd shell it can't be erased. Like most designers who pyro-engrave, you may want to first sketch the design on the gourd shell with a pencil or chalk and then burn in the outline of the design. After completing the pyrography, wash or erase the drawn lines so that you can see how the design and the gourd shell work together.

NANCY TELLO

FREE-HAND WOOD BURNING

Duane Teeter is one artist who prefers to wood burn designs on a gourd without using predrawn lines or patterns. Many of his designs start with a base point: he identifies the center of the pattern and then burns four marks to indicate the principal compass points. These points are then connected and embellished with a variety of scrolls, dashes, lines, and shapes. As the design expands, it does not always remain symmetrical; however, it's always balanced to complement the shape of the gourd itself.

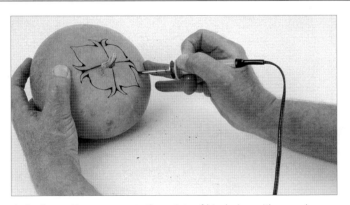

Artist Duane Teeter connects the points of his design with curved or straight lines to create zones that are balanced.

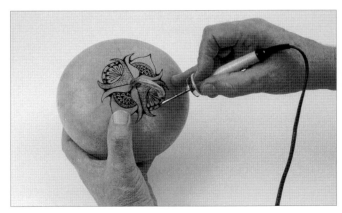

He fills in spaces with a variety of lines, dots, and shading, all with the same wood-burning tip.

JENNIFER LOE

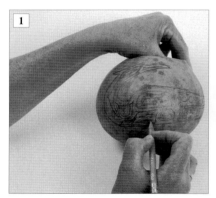

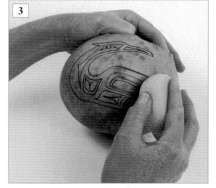

COMPLETING A DESIGN

Once the basic outline of a design is burned into the gourd, there are several different ways to complete it.

1. The design can be left alone as an outline, similar to a pen-and-ink sketch. The general-purpose tip can be used to burn in light lines for shading or deeper and darker lines for emphasis. By using the side of the tip or by turning it upside down, different types of shading and marks can be created.

2. To create depth and coloration, specialized tips and variations in burning techniques can be used.

3. The wood-burned lines can serve as an outline that can be painted or stained. The wood burning itself is an effective barrier or dam that prevents stains or paints from bleeding into each other. This combination of pyrography and coloring is used a great deal by many artists today.

Wood Burned and Stained Bowl

The design on this attractive bowl, created with a basic wood-burning tool, was enhanced with leather dyes.

WHAT YOU NEED

Gourd with a smooth surface, cured and cleaned
Power or hand cutting tool
Sandpaper
Black leather dye
Pencil or chalk
Wood-burning tool
Damp sponge
Small paintbrush
Leather stains, dyes, or inks
Clear furniture or floor wax
Soft cloth

WHAT YOU DO

1. Cut an opening in the gourd and remove the pulp and seeds. Sand the cut edge smooth.

2. Stain the inside of the gourd and the cut edge with the black leather dye and let dry overnight.

3. Use the pencil or chalk to lightly draw your design on the gourd (Photo 1).

4. Wood burn the penciled design, using even pressure to create smooth lines (Photo 2).

5. Wash off the pencil or chalk marks with a damp sponge (Photo 3).

6. With a small paintbrush, color in the design with leather stains, dyes, or inks (Photo 4). Allow the gourd to dry overnight, then apply several coats of wax or polish to protect the gourd surface and give it a soft luster.

JUDY MULFORD
Pandanus Preparation
PHOTO BY ARTIST

HAL HALL
COLLECTION OF VIRGINIA CUNNINGHAM

LUPE MOLINA *Coyote Gourds on Joshua Tree Stands* PHOTO BY BRIAN RENNIE

RIDGE KUNZEL *Madonna* COLLECTION OF LINDA LINDBERG

RIDGE KUNZEL AND ROY SCHICK
Raven with Dr

KERRY AND JAMIE DEVRIENT, Terra Nova Gourdworks
Lily and Pansy Silhouette Botanical Box
COLLECTION OF GINGER SUMMIT

NAN TOOTHMAN
Market Madonna
PHOTO BY KAREN A. BAGGOTT

CAROLYN RUSHTON
PHOTO BY BEVERLY J. STULL

OTHER PYROGRAPHY METHODS

Like a traditional gourd artist in New Guinea and Peru, you can burn the surface of a gourd using a direct flame or heat source. Instead of a glowing eucalyptus stick, you can use a pen-size propane torch; by moving it across the gourd shell, you can shade thin lines and small areas. Because of the intense heat generated by these torches, be sure to wear a leather glove on the hand holding the gourd.

Gourds can also be toasted in the oven to achieve an overall darker color. Oil the gourd surface first with mineral or safflower oil and then place it on the lowest rack of a 200°F (92°C) oven. Watch the gourd carefully and turn it often so it doesn't burn unevenly. After ten minutes, remove the gourd from the oven, check the condition of the shell, and reapply the oil. You can also place a gourd under the broiler, resting on the lowest oven shelf. You'll need to watch the gourd constantly; only the surface closest to the broiler will darken, making it possible to selectively control the scorched areas. Any gourd that has been scorched or toasted should be treated with a mineral oil to restore some of the moisture and luster to its surface.

Carving

HISTORICAL OVERVIEW

For thousands of years, crafters in cultures around the world have engraved and carved designs on gourds. The oldest known embellished gourd, encircled with carved patterns, is from the coastal Huaca Prieta site in northern Peru, dating from 2500 B.C. Engraved gourds from locations as diverse as China, South America, Africa, and Hawaii depict scenes of daily life, images from nature and mythology, and sacred or religious symbols. These images often provide the anthropologist and historian with important clues about the social and political events and supernatural beliefs that filled the lives of people from ages past.

The tools that were used to engrave the gourds were very simple—a sharp point from a tooth, or a bone or metal tip imbedded in a wooden handle. In Asia, needles were used to engrave exquisite detail on gourds. In Peru and Africa, metal points resembling sharpened nails and screwdrivers were secured in wood or bamboo handles and used for carving. Despite the crudeness of the tools, the level of detail displayed on many of the very old engraved gourds is rarely matched in gourd carving today.

Initially, the designs that were scratched, pressed, or scraped into a gourd surface were difficult to see and became visible only after the entire surface of the gourd was rubbed with a dark substance. In Peru and West Africa, the gourd was rubbed with charcoal made from burning grasses that were mixed with heated grease, oil, or animal fat. The Frafra people in Bolgatanga in northern Ghana rub the black-brown oil from the Shee nut into designs scratched with an awl. In China, the gourd was rubbed with lamp black or carbon-based inks. Once the shell was polished, the dark pigments remained in the engraved lines and the surface of the gourd shell retained a burnished polish. As universal as fine-line engraving was in ages past, this style of gourd carving is rarely used today.

Large gourd containers from East Africa are frequently scratched with elaborate images of wildlife and other natural scenes. The background is filled in with cross-hatching or small designs. The entire gourd is rubbed with betelnut or charcoal mixed with grease to blacken the design and burnish the gourd shell.

COLLECTION OF GINGER SUMMIT

This small gourd from China is engraved with images of the constellations.

COLLECTION OF JIM WIDESS

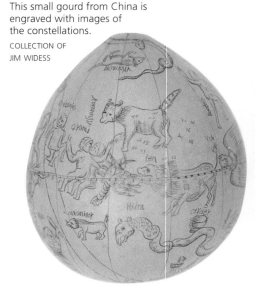

Tree gourd from the Philippines circa 1898 was engraved with elaborate designs and left untreated.

COLLECTION OF DAVID KING

After it was carved, the designs on this Peruvian platter were scorched to accent areas and details.

This Peruvian gourd depicts mining activities. Once carved, the gourd was rubbed with charcoal left from burning grasses mixed with hot grease, to blacken the background.

In addition to finely engraved designs, most early cultures throughout the world also used several other forms of carving. Detailed scenes of rural or village life, animals or natural images, or important cultural symbols were outlined into the gourd shell and the background was then removed. Occasionally, the entire gourd was stained prior to carving; in Peru, gourds were sometimes soaked in a dye bath of purple, red, or green (see page 58). The carved lines appear white against this colored shell. In most instances, however, the shell may have been darkened slightly with an oil; once carved, the gourd was usually left untreated. Examples of this type of carving are found from such diverse locales as Mexico, Peru, Africa, and the Philippines.

In Peru and also in some cultures in Africa, the carved designs on the gourd shell were often scorched after the carving was finished, thus increasing the contrast and the visibility of the image. Another method used to highlight the carved image was to lighten or darken the background. To darken the background of the exposed shell, a mixture of grease and charcoal was rubbed into the carved areas; to make it lighter, the areas were filled with crushed chalk.

Today, some tribes in Western Africa, notably in Ghana and Nigeria, carve gourds with very deep lines, occasionally penetrating the shell. Using a curved metal knife similar to a linoleum cutter, geometric shapes are sculpted into the gourd shell to form edges, wedges, flowing patterns, or open lattice work.

On this small tree gourd canteen from Costa Rica, more of the background shell has been removed, compared to the carved gourds of other countries.

COLLECTION OF CHRIS HOBACK

CONTEMPORARY CARVING TOOLS

Because of the many types of carving tools that are available today and the diversity among artists using them, contemporary gourd carvings are quite different from those of other cultures and other times. Today's artists use hand chisels, knives and gouges, and hand-held power tools. A basic craft or hobby knife works well, too, and comes with a variety of interchangeable blades and tips. Woodworking gouges can be purchased individually or in sets and come in many different shapes and sizes; handles, shanks, and cutting edges are available to meet almost any carving requirement. Regardless of the tool selected, it's important to keep the blades sharp: This is important not only to prolong the life of the tool and ease the carving task, but for safety reasons as well.

Several hand-held power tools are also available, which come with a wide choice of interchangeable tips. Although several manufacturers produce these tools, three forms of power tools are particularly suitable for working on gourds: 1) a small hand-held unit attached by a cord to a separate power pack, 2) a portable unit with a rechargeable battery, and 3) a flexible hose attached to a motor that can be hung or rested on a stand. To meet different carving needs, many accessories can be purchased for each of these units whether you're making the initial slice in the gourd shell, completing the finishing details, or sanding surfaces and edges. (See Supply Sources on page 142.)

LORRAINE ZIELINSKI

GINGER SUMMIT

SELECTING A GOURD

In selecting a gourd for carving, look for one with a thick and uniform surface, free from blemishes or tightly curved surfaces. A thick shell is important for two reasons: 1) when you carve into the surface, you want to avoid cutting completely through the shell, and 2) the carving tool often exerts very concentrated pressure on a shell and may crack a gourd with a thin shell. Sometimes it's difficult to determine the thickness of the shell before you actually cut into it. Look for gourds that are heavy relative to their size. Tapping or thumping on a gourd can give you a rather subtle clue; compare several gourds until you are able to feel and hear a difference in their shell resonance. Also, look for a fresh shiny shell that can't be pierced or dented with a fingernail or pencil point; older and softer shells do not carve well.

The curved slick surface of the gourd is the biggest hurdle to gourd carving. Several hints may help to stabilize the gourd and protect you from a tool that might skitter or slip on the gourd surface.

1. Wear a leather apron if you are going to hold the gourd on your lap.

2. Place the gourd on a foam pad that will grip the gourd securely on a working surface or on your lap.

3. Wear a rubber or leather glove on the hand that is holding the gourd.

4. If a gourd surface is extremely hard to carve, try soaking the gourd in water for a period of time to soften the shell slightly.

ELIZABETH LOFTUS
PHOTO BY DIANE STANTON

CARVING TECHNIQUES

Most artists use a pencil to sketch a design onto the gourd; then they carve out the design and rub or wash away the pencil lines. You can also lightly wood burn the outline of the design. The wood-burned edge helps to define the design and provides a precise and smooth definition between the surface and the background. However, once a design is wood burned into the shell, it's difficult to change.

Before you start to carve, you need to decide whether or not you want to darken the shell with either stain or paint; a stained or painted shell stands out in greater contrast to the relatively light inner shell. If, prior to carving, you decide to paint the shell with an opaque paint, you'll need to wood burn the design so that you can still see the outline.

There are two fundamental styles of carving: One is that the background negative space is carved away from the design; the other is that the design itself is carved into the surface. Decide which style to use before you start to carve.

Once you have considered these options, you are ready to begin carving. Keep in mind that although the surface of the shell may be quite dense, the inner shell is relatively soft. Carve, chip, or scrape away the outer skin first with a very shallow cut, and then gradually carve away the inner shell to the depth you choose. Proceed carefully, for shells can be thinner in some parts than others. The exposed under-shell can be sanded smooth or left rough, depending on your design.

LORRAINE ZIELINSKI

DR. LESLIE MILLER

JOHN HORNE
This gourd was stained after it was carved to darken the background shell.
PHOTO BY ARTIST

USING A HAND GOUGE

The design for this piece, inspired by carved bowls from Suriname, was drawn and wood burned into the surface. Using a gouge tip from an interchangeable hobby knife set, the blade was pressed firmly into the gourd shell to make the initial cut. Then, the gouge was gently pushed under the surface of the gourd shell with a rocking motion. The exterior shell was removed with short gouging motions. Once the background had been completely exposed, it was smoothed with sandpaper. The completed platter was oiled to protect the exposed shell. Intended for regular use as a serving dish, the interior was treated with vegetable oil to season and seal the porous shell.

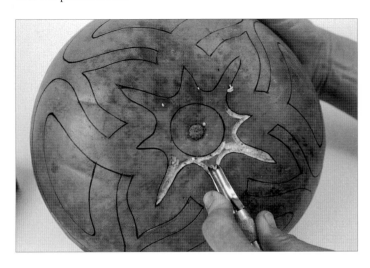

Halloween Gourd

Instead of decorating a pumpkin this year, why not carve this fanciful gourd? Complete with a witch flying over the moon, the gourd will last for dozens of Halloweens.

WHAT YOU NEED

Gourd (pumpkin shaped), cured and washed
Pencil
Sharp knife
Power or hand cutting tool
Sandpaper
Paintbrush
Orange leather dye
Metallic copper acrylic paint
Power hand tool with a small burr and a
 larger round-headed burr
Black leather dye
Mineral or salad oil
Black enamel spray paint

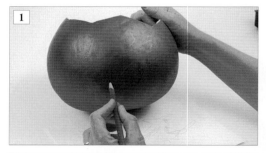

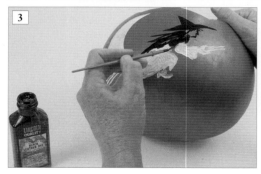

WHAT YOU DO

1. With the pencil, mark a zig-zag line for cutting the top off the gourd much as you would cut a pumpkin. Make an initial slice with the knife and then carefully saw along the lines with the hand or power cutting tool. Remove the pulp and seeds and sand the interior and the cut edge smooth.

2. Paint the gourd, including the lid, with orange leather dye and let dry overnight. Then, rub the surface with a coat of thinned metallic copper paint and let dry overnight.

3. Lightly draw the design onto the gourd (Photo 1).

4. With the small bit, carve the outline of the design. Use the larger round-headed bit to scrape away the larger surface areas (Photo 2). Carve the entire design. Because of the strong color contrast between the exterior and the interior gourd shell, carve just deep enough to remove the colored outer skin. The surface of the carved area can be textured or shaped to complement the design. Here, the witch's hair and dress were textured to suggest the flow of wind.

5. Color all or a portion of the design with black leather dye (Photo 3). In this example, the witch is darkened and the moon is left pale, both providing a sharp contrast against the orange shell. Allow the dye to dry overnight and then oil the exposed shell.

6. Spray the interior of the gourd black.

DR. LESLIE MILLER
This gourd was carved with a hand gouge, and only portions of the shell were stained so that the complex arrangement of stars is dramatically revealed.
PHOTO BY
DOYLE YODER

INLAY

Inlay is an embellishment technique that is closely related to carving. After a portion of the outer shell has been carved out, it can be filled with a wide variety of materials. Frequently, a stone such as turquoise or coral is set in the shell as a special accent or focus for the design. You can also carve away a larger area of the gourd surface and fill it with metal shapes, shells, or chips of stones. A mosaic can be created with chipped tile or beads.

Before you begin an inlay project, select a gourd with a shell that is thick enough so that an indentation can be carved into it without penetrating all the way through the shell or weakening the overall gourd. If the surface is to be dyed, stained, or otherwise embellished, complete that work first before starting the inlay carving.

Trace the object to be set in the gourd shell. Using hand or power tools, remove the outer skin of the gourd shell. The depth of carving depends on the effect you wish to achieve. If you want the material to protrude above the surface level of the shell, you need to carve only deep enough to accommodate the adhesive and the base of the inlay. If you want the new inlay to be even with the gourd surface, carve the area deep enough to allow for the adhesive plus the material. Occasionally, stop carving and place the object in the space you are creating for it to make sure you do not carve away more than necessary and accidentally penetrate the shell.

SUZYE OGAWA AND JOSEPH ADDOTTA

STAINING OPTIONS

To darken the exposed shell, you may want to stain the gourd after only part of the design is carved. Any carving that is done after the staining can either remain pale or be colored with a different stain. Ornate patterns can be created by varying the sequence of staining and carving (see Leslie Miller's dramatic gourd, above).

If only the background is to be carved, you can remove the entire background surrounding the design or texture the area with a repeated gouged pattern. The carved area can be left neutral, which will remain pale against the gourd shell, or can be filled in with a stain or paint. Once a background is removed, additional details can be carved into your design.

The type of adhesive to use will depend on the materials you are going to set. Wood glues are suitable for most objects. Super-glues and resin glues provide an extra strong bond for holding special stones or objects.

After the adhesive is completely set and the new material is anchored firmly in place, fill in around the periphery of the object with a grout of wood putty or modeling clay to even the surface as well as to provide additional security for the inlay. A touch-up with polish is usually all that is necessary to guarantee a beautiful accent to the gourd design.

LIZ CUNNINGHAM
PHOTO BY GEORGE POST

GINGER SUMMIT
Sections of the shell were removed so that the copper pieces can lie flush with the shell.

DEBORAH MARTINEZ RAMBEAU
Centered
PHOTO HARRY BACH

LATTICE CUTTING

Another decorative technique related to carving requires cutting or carving through the gourd shell in such a way that the open spaces become part of the design and the interior surface of the gourd becomes visually important. The eye is drawn to the negative space; the contrasts between the exterior and interior surfaces are integrated in the total design of the gourd.

For this approach, select a gourd that has a smooth, even, and strong shell. It's not necessary for the shell to be thick as in other carving techniques, but it must be strong enough to withstand the pressure of cutting and sanding. Depending on the complexity of the cutouts, it's usually easier and safer to thoroughly clean the interior before the spaces are cut away. You may also spray or color the gourd interior prior to cutting the shell, so that any colors applied to the inner surfaces do not drip on the exterior shell.

STEVE AND SUE BUCK

LISA LARRIBA
Four Lizards

SHEILA SATOW
Festival Table Lamp
Slits cut into the gourd are backed with colored plastic to create an interesting lamp.

GAIL AND TIM YOUNGBLUTH
Fretwork Gourd

Potpourri Holder

This simple project demonstrates lattice carving. Fill the container with your favorite potpourri.

WHAT YOU NEED

Round or tobacco box gourd with a smooth
    shell, cured and washed
Pencil
Wood-burning tool
Power drill with 1/4-inch (0.6 cm) bit
Small power saw or hobby jigsaw
Sharp knife
Fine-toothed saw
Sandpaper
Hand-held power tool with sanding attachment
    or small files
Paintbrushes
Leather dyes in red, green, orange, and brown
Varnish
Potpourri

WHAT YOU DO

1. Draw the leaf patterns onto the gourd surface so that they overlap and, once cut, will create open spaces. For ease of cutting, the leaves should have relatively simple outlines. Pencil in the line where you will cut to create the lid; the cut will be less visible and the lid will fit better if the line dips and curves slightly.

2. Use the wood-burning tool to engrave the design into the gourd. Drill holes in the spaces between the leaf patterns that will be removed, including the larger area at the top of the gourd (Photo 1).

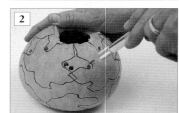

3. Using a small power saw or hobby jigsaw, remove the portion at the top of the gourd. Clean out some of the seeds and inner pulp before cutting out the smaller spaces between the leaves (Photo 2).

4. Use the knife to make a small slit along the cutting line between the lid and the bottom of the gourd; then, with the fine-toothed saw, cut along this line. Lift off the lid and remove the remaining pulp and seeds. Sand the interior smooth. Don't sand the actual cut edge because you want to keep a close fit between the lid and the base.

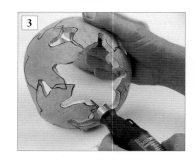

5. Sand the cut edges between the leaves with sandpaper, small files, or a hand-held power tool with a sanding attachment. Some lattice designs are emphasized by painting the edges a contrasting color. Here, the edges were beveled with a motorized file so that the lines of the design appear sharp against the interior space (Photo 3).

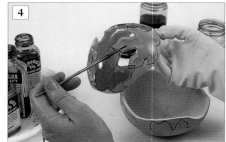

6. Color in the design with leather dyes (Photo 4). You can tint or paint the interior in a color that contrasts or complements the design. Let the gourd dry overnight. Then apply a light coat of varnish on the interior and exterior surfaces.

7. Let the container dry overnight and fill it with your favorite potpourri.

DESIGNING WITH A DRILL

Some gourd designs are created simply by drilling holes in the gourd shell. Early American settlers often used a dipper gourd that was perforated with many holes as a sieve, either to water plants or to sift and sort dry materials. Gourd lanterns used by early settlers and Native Americans were made by perforating the sides and then partially filling the interior with sand to hold a candle. If you put a candle inside a gourd, be sure the candle is encased in a glass container and will not be covered by a gourd lid. Remember that gourds are flammable and can be potential fire hazards.

Many people use gourds as lamp shades or coverings over light bulbs. Holes can be combined with slits cut in the gourd shell; when these spaces are covered with a colored plastic, the lamp provides an interesting play of light and color. The hardware that is necessary to attach the shade to the lamp can be purchased at hardware or specialty lamp stores (see examples on page 93). Be sure that the gourd shell is far enough away from the light bulb so that the shell doesn't singe or burn. Also, be sure to have plenty of holes or open spaces in the upper part of the gourd so that the hot air can escape safely. Use a low wattage bulb.

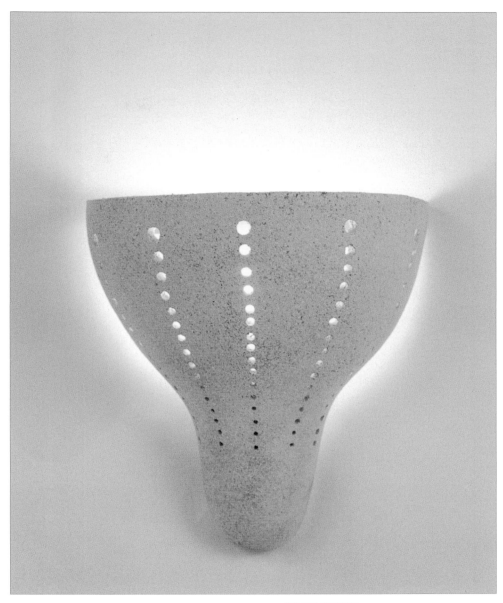

GINGER SUMMIT

This wall sconce was drilled with holes of varying diameter to create simple patterns. Metal brackets fastened to the back of the gourd provide support for the light fixture.

Use of a drill alone can create interesting patterns in a gourd shell.

GOURD BIRDHOUSES AND BIRDFEEDERS

Another reason to drill holes in a gourd is to make a home for birds. There are a number of excellent books that describe how to make gourd birdhouses. The American Gourd Society also has information that will help you determine what type and size gourd you need for the kind of bird you hope to attract (see Supply Sources on page 142). Most birds are quite particular about the size of the opening in a prospective home, as well as the dimensions of the interior. Here are a few examples of gourd birdhouses and one nicely carved feeder.

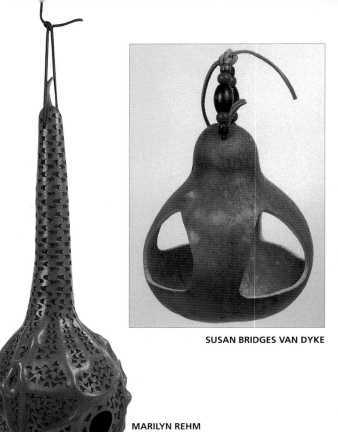

SUSAN BRIDGES VAN DYKE

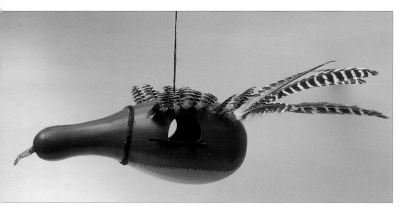

PAM BARTON *Sapper* PHOTO BY SHERI SIEGEL

MARILYN HOST

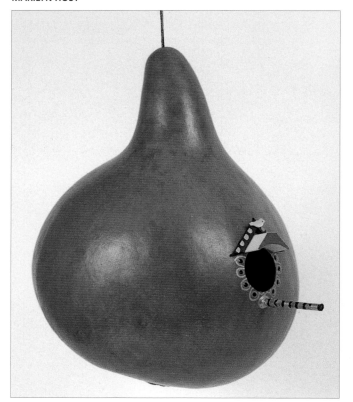

MARILYN REHM

BILL KUPKA
House wren entering
maranka gourd birdhouse
PHOTO BY ARTIST

Chapter Five

BASKETRY
AND
WEAVING

DON WEEKE

HISTORICAL OVERVIEW

Many of the very oldest gourd fragments found near the remains of human settlements all over the world have been wrapped in some form of cordage or netting made from vines, reed, sinew, or leather strips. The cordage may have served a utilitarian or protective function or purely as a decoration. Although some of the gourds were attached to fishing nets, others had cords carefully fastened around them. Net slings and pouches made gourds more convenient for transporting food and supplies, and also gave people a way to hang them out of reach of animals or other pests. In several cultures, baskets continue to be tightly woven around gourds to cover them completely. In Niger and Nigeria, these serve to carry, protect, and store a woman's valuable dowry gourds. In Japan, reed baskets protect and balance sake bottles the farmers carry into the fields. In Hawaii, storage trunks are made of two separate very large gourds laced together, each completely covered with basketry.

The Zulu tribe in Africa is well recognized for its excellent craftsmanship with beads. Clothing, jewelry, and household objects are covered with ornate beaded designs. Beadwork also decorates gourds of all shapes and sizes; often the gourd is completely obscured by beads.

The interior of a gourd hat worn by farmers in the Philippines was filled with an elaborate plaited head support. COLLECTION OF EUGENIA GWATHNEY

Small gourds are completely hidden by fancy beadwork on these Zulu, South African pieces. COLLECTION OF CAROL MORRISON

Cords were woven around this 19th century Columbian container so that it could be carried or hung on hooks inside the house.
CASA ANTIGUA, REDWOOD CITY, CALIFORNIA.

GINGER SUMMIT
Plaiting is used to embellish this gourd.

Wrapping

The simplest way to cover or reinforce a gourd shell is by simply wrapping it with another material, such as cord, twine, leather strips, raffia, etc. You can completely cover the gourd or wrap just a portion, such as the neck. In either case, you need to first roughen with sandpaper or a file the area to be covered and then coat it with an adhesive, such as wood glue or all-purpose resin glue.

To begin the wrapping, anchor the end of the material to the gourd shell by poking a hole in the shell and gluing the end in place. Or, you can hide the end under successive rows of wrapping. Wrap the material around the gourd, pulling it taut so that it fits snugly against the rows already in place. Then, taper the end of the material and force it under the wrapped area; use a bit of glue to insure it won't pull free. After the adhesive has dried completely, the gourd can be coated with a varnish or clear-drying adhesive, or painted with an acrylic paint. The finish serves to further secure the material to the gourd surface.

NANCY LEE SCHLENDER
The neck and base of this gourd decanter are wrapped with jute.

Coiling

Coiling is the most frequently used method to embellish the neck of a gourd. Coiling can be as simple as attaching a single layer of material around the neck of a gourd with an overhand stitch or as elaborate as building up the base with a basketry extension, such as Don Weeke's gourd on page 97.

Although the stitches securing the coil in place can be plain or fancy, the basic coiling technique is quite easy. Any kind of material can be used as the foundation for the coil: pine needles, twine or cord, vines, twisted fabric, leather strips, to name a few. You also have great flexibility in the choice of material to use for lacing the coil. Waxed linen is frequently used because it is strong, durable, readily available, and comes in a variety of colors. Twine, raffia, leather, and even thin wire can be used. No matter what materials you use, it's important to finish the gourd surface before starting the basketry (see Exterior Finishes on page 33).

R.K. HEJNY

PHOTO BY DREW DONOVAN

Examples of Coiling

DEBORA MUHL
Afternoon Tea

CHRIS HOBACK

DEB ABRAHAMSON

MARY HETTMANSPERGER

JERRALDINE MASTEN HANSEN
PHOTO BY GREG WUTKE

GAYNA URANSKY   *A Woman's Basket*   PHOTO BY ARTIST

KRIS THOENI

Coiled Basket with Beads

A simple overhand stitch was used to attach the date palm to this gourd, but the effect is stunning.

WHAT YOU NEED

Gourd, cured and cleaned
Sharp knife
Power or hand cutting tool
Sandpaper
Electric drill with 1/16-inch (1.5 mm) bit
   or leather awl
Neutral-colored shoe polish
1/4 pound (110 g) date palm fruiting stalks
Bowl of water
Tapestry needle
Brown waxed linen thread
Basketry clippers or garden shears
Masking tape
30 small beads with holes large enough for the
   date palm to fit through

WHAT YOU DO

1. Cut an opening in the gourd; it can be regular or very curved, depending on the shape of the gourd and your own design preference. Remove the pulp and seeds and sand smooth the interior and the cut edge.

2. With a drill or leather awl, makes holes around the opening just large enough to accommodate the needle and lacing material. Drill the holes approximately 1/2 inch (1.3 cm) apart.

3. Treat and finish the gourd shell with several coats of neutral-colored shoe polish.

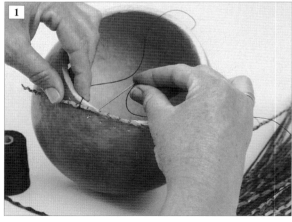

4. Soak the date palm in water for about 15 minutes so that it will more easily conform to the curvature of the opening. With one hand, hold some of the date palm against the top edge of the gourd neck. Starting inside the gourd, insert the threaded needle through a hole and pull the thread around and over the date palm (see Photo 1). Proceed to the next hole and pull each stitch taut. Use an overhand stitch: loop the thread over the coil and insert the needle through the next hole in the gourd shell. (If you pinch the thread firmly in place as you bring it over the coil, you can create a vertical pattern as you add more coils.)

5. To create a fringe of date palm, add a new piece with each stitch. If the coil gets too thick, cut away some of the thick ends of the previous pieces (see Photo 2).

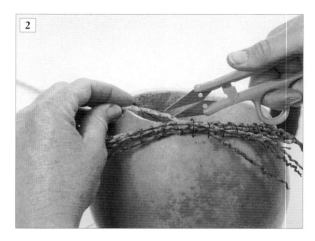

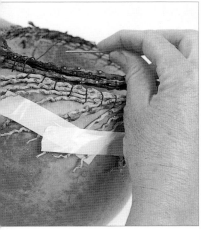

6. If you want to cover only the edge of the gourd with a single layer of date palm, taper the ends of the coil so they can be tucked behind the beginning of the row to create an even surface. Knot the lacing thread when the ends of the date palm are secured and bury the thread in the coil. Use masking tape to hold the fringe ends of the date palm secure against the gourd and out of the way of the coiling (see Photo 3).

7. If you want to build up more layers as was done here, keep adding rows of coil on top of the first row. When you begin the second row, put the needle through the center of the first coiled row, next to the stitch, instead of through a hole in the gourd (see Photo 4).

8. Some ends of the date palm are thick and stiff. Cut them off when necessary to maintain a flexible coil (see Photo 5).

9. Add new pieces of date palm to keep the coil a consistent diameter (see Photo 6).

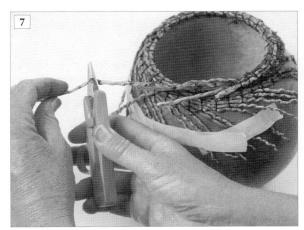

10. When you have added as many rows as you want, cut the ends of the date palm to a gentle taper so that the final row creates a smooth edge (see Photo 7).

11. Work the final ends of date palm behind the last row of coiling and secure the lacing thread with a knot, burying the end in the coil (see Photo 8).

12. To finish, thread the small beads onto the date palm fringe.

■ *There are many excellent books available that provide detailed instructions on coiling materials, techniques, and variations that can be adapted for embellishing gourds. We particularly like* Fiber Basketry, Homegrown and Handmade *(Kangaroo Press, 1989), because of its emphasis on using garden materials for coiled basketry.*

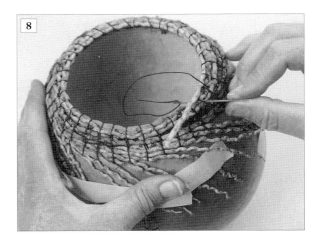

Couching

Couching, another simple embellishment technique, is accomplished by tacking some type of thread, cord, or other material onto the gourd surface. If the material is stiff, soak it for up to 15 minutes so that it can conform to the shape of the gourd and then blot it dry so that it won't mar the shell.

CAROLA FARTHING
A black cord is couched in a spiral around the gourd body and each stitch secures a small bead or gourd seed.

BEVERLY SHAMANA
Date palm has been dyed and couched onto the surface of this gourd vessel.

JUDY MULFORD
Ceremonial Gourd
In addition to the pine needles couched on the exterior of this gourd, a coiled pine needle basket is enclosed inside.
PHOTO BY ARTIST

Gourd with Philodendron Sheaths

This gourd is couched with the reddish-brown sheaths that protect the emerging frond of the giant philodendron plant. Their color and texture harmonize beautifully with the gourd surface.

WHAT YOU NEED

Gourd, cured and cleaned
Power or hand cutting tool
Sandpaper
Neutral-colored shoe polish
Pencil
Electric drill with 1/16-inch
   (1.5 mm) bit or leather awl
Masking tape
Tapestry needle
Waxed linen thread
3 philodendron sheaths
   (see basketry sources on
   page 142)
2 jacaranda pods (or other pods)
Beads

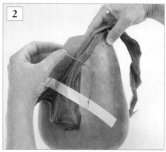

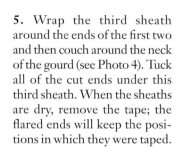

WHAT YOU DO

1. Cut an opening in the gourd and remove the pulp and seeds. Sand smooth the interior and the cut edge. Apply several coats of neutral-colored shoe polish to the outside surface.

2. Draw a line on the shell where the materials are to be added and use the drill or leather awl to make holes along this line (see Photo 1). When couching thin materials such as vine, insert the threaded needle through a hole, wrap the material, and then insert the needle through the same hole. When couching thicker materials such as these sheaths, make pairs of holes, one on either side of the line, so that you can hold the material flat against the gourd. Make only as many holes as are necessary to hold the material securely in place.

3. Soak the sheaths in water for about five minutes or until they are soft and pliable. Position a sheath against the gourd and hold it in place with masking tape. Pull the threaded needle through the first hole and bury the knot under the sheath. Bring the needle out of the hole on the opposite side of the sheath and enter the first hole again, pulling the thread taut to hold the sheath in place (see Photo 2).

4. Continue to stitch the sheath stem to the gourd. Hold the second sheath in place with a bit of tape while you stitch it down (see Photo 3). The distance between the stitches will vary depending on the material being added and the path along which it is being secured. You may need to reinforce the couching

with a bit of glue if the material is particularly stiff or heavy.

5. Wrap the third sheath around the ends of the first two and then couch around the neck of the gourd (see Photo 4). Tuck all of the cut ends under this third sheath. When the sheaths are dry, remove the tape; the flared ends will keep the positions in which they were taped.

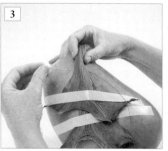

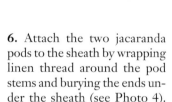

6. Attach the two jacaranda pods to the sheath by wrapping linen thread around the pod stems and burying the ends under the sheath (see Photo 4). Attach the beads with thread that is anchored in one of the holes.

Twining

A different type of basketry technique, twining, can also be used to build up the neck of a gourd container. Twining is the process of twisting two or more weavers around the warp or spokes to build up a solid container.

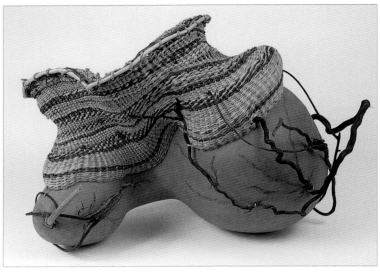

DEBORAH MOSKOWITZ *She's All Curves*
These spokes were brought through holes made in the sides of the gourd around the rim and then bent upwards.

DENISE WIND WALKER *Coyote's Nest*
The bone spokes for this twining were fastened on the gourd shell first and then twined to hold them firmly in place.

JOHN MCGUIRE Twill work   PHOTO BY ARTIST

EVA WALSH *By The Sea*   PHOTO BY RANDALL SMITH

Twined Gourd Bowl

Use only a thick-shelled gourd for this project so that you can drill holes in the lip.

WHAT YOU NEED

Thick-shelled gourd, cured and cleaned
Power or hand cutting tool
Sandpaper
Leather dyes in two colors that complement
   the twining material
Paintbrush
Varnish
Basketry or commercial dye
1 pound (454 g) #3 round reed, 1/8-inch
   (2.25 mm) in diameter
Electric drill with a 1/8-inch (2.25 mm) bit
Basketry clippers or pruning shears
Carpenter's glue or craft glue
Masking tape
Coconut fiber or thick yarn or cord
   in two colors
Bucket of warm water
Round-nose pliers

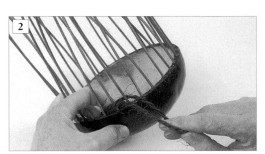

WHAT YOU DO

1. Cut the gourd open to the desired size and remove the pulp and seeds. Sand smooth the interior and the cut edge. Stain the gourd shell with both colors of leather dye to create a marbled effect. When dry, apply a coat of varnish and let the gourd dry overnight.

2. Dye the round reed, according to the manufacturer's directions.

3. Drill holes that exactly match the diameter of the reed, 1/2 inch (1.3 cm) apart into the lip of the gourd. Cut spokes of reed 12 inches (30.5 cm) long and glue them into the holes. Glue the spokes firmly in place and allow to dry overnight.

4. To begin twining, tape the ends of two weavers on the inside of the gourd and bring the long ends through the spaces on each side of one spoke (see Photo 1). If you are using only one color of twining material, you can simply fold one weaver in half around one spoke, thus creating two working ends.

5. Bring the weaver on the left (the left-hand weaver) in front of the first spoke to the right and weave it behind and around the second spoke (see Photo 2). Now the new strand is the left-hand weaver. Bring this weaver in front of the adjacent right-hand spoke and above and behind the next spoke (see Photo 3). You will see that the two weavers have twisted around each other.

6. Keep twining the weavers around the spokes in this manner until the desired height is reached (see Photo 4). Allow at least an additional 6 to 8 inches (15 to 20 cm) for the finishing border. As you weave, you can adjust the shape of the basket by manipulating each spoke after you have twined around it. By pulling each spoke toward you as you complete each twined stitch around the spoke, you will gradually flare the basket out. By straightening each spoke, the basket wall will remain straight. By pushing each spoke inward, the basket will begin to narrow. Keep the rows of twining packed as you weave.

7. Add new twining material as necessary, keeping the short ends inside the gourd; these can be trimmed when the weaving is complete. This basket has nine rows of twining.

8. Now you are ready to finish the top edge. Hold the basket upside down in a bucket of warm water for five minutes; this soaking will make the spokes more pliable and less likely to split.

9. With the round-nose pliers, crimp the spokes next to the top row of twining so that they will bend easily without breaking. Choose any spoke and fold it down behind the next two spokes to the right. Then bring the end out to the front of the basket between the third and fourth spokes. Do the same with all of the remaining spoke ends (see Photo 5).

10. When you are folding down the next to the last spoke, carefully work the end behind and through the space between the first and second spoke (see Photo 6). Do the same with the last spoke, working it into the space between the second and third spoke. Now all of the spokes should be bent down and secure, pointing to the outside of the basket. If the spokes are made of a natural material, metal wire, or other interesting texture, you may want to leave the ends projecting out in this manner, or just cut them short and fringe the ends. If you want a more finished braid for the edge, you need to work the ends of the spokes back to the inside of the basket. To do so, take the first spoke and work the end under the loop that has been created between the third and fourth spokes (see Photo 7). Pull it tight, and hold it down against the edge of the inside of the basket as you pull the loops taut over it (see Photo 8). Continue to work all the ends of the spokes back to the inside of the basket edge.

11. Allow the project to dry overnight before trimming the ends of the spokes. Natural materials such as round reed will shrink as they dry, and you want to make sure the ends are secure before they are trimmed.

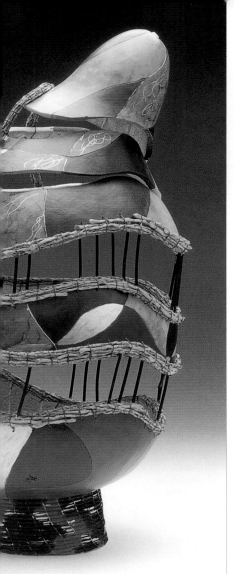

GINGER SUMMIT

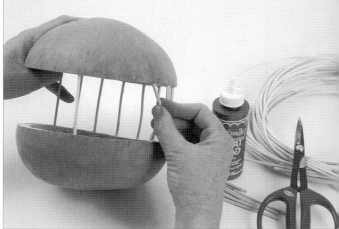

Split Gourd

The split gourd technique is similar to the twining method described above but both ends of the spokes are anchored in two halves of a gourd (see photo above). The spokes can be woven or twined with a different material, or they can be left bare, painted, or decorated with randomly placed beads. If the spokes themselves are an interesting material, such as bent twigs or date palm, the contrast with the gourd shell can be very effective.

When making a split gourd design, you want to be sure to draw a line where the gourd will be cut in two. Before you actually cut the gourd, mark the places where the holes for the spokes will be drilled and where the two halves of the gourd should be realigned. This step is important, because once the gourd is cut in half, you want to be able to realign the holes exactly over each other.

If you want to use the twining technique to weave materials around the spokes, it doesn't matter how many spokes you have. The space between the spokes is determined by the thickness and the flexibility of the material that you use for the twining. If you're planning to weave materials around the spokes (that is use one weaver to alternately go in front of or behind each spoke) make sure you have an odd number of spokes.

EVA WALSH   *Spirits Rising*   PHOTO BY RANDALL SMITH

Slit Weaving

Slits can be cut into the sides of the gourd so that the shell itself becomes the warp or the spokes for the twining or weaving. Be sure the slits are cut wide enough to accommodate the materials you have selected to weave through the gourd shell. If you plan to use the twining technique described above, it doesn't matter how many or how wide the spaces between the slits are. However, if you plan to weave material into the gourd one end at a time, then you must have an odd number of slits. This is essential so that the second row of weaving will be opposite the first row, thus filling all of the spaces by passing alternately in front of or behind the gourd shell.

GINGER SUMMIT
Slits were cut into the sides of the gourd and then seagrass cordage was woven in the spokes to create a gourd basket.

ORLANDO HERNANDEZ

Designs can be quite elaborate, depending on the color and placement of the beads.

BOB PATTERSON

Netting

Throughout the world gourds have been carried, protected, and stored in net bags or slings. In Hawaii, loose netting was secured to the bottom of a gourd and then brought over the top of a second gourd and tied in a knot to hold both gourds together and secure. To make a loose netting or sling that will fit around a gourd, first secure several cords together around a center loop or metal ring. Then tie adjoining strands together with a simple overhand knot, square knot, or netting knot. For each row of knots, tie alternate pairs of cords until the desired length of netting is reached. The ends of the cords can be tied together to create a handle from which to suspend the gourd, or they can be secured to a ring or loop of cord that is fastened at the upper edge of the gourd so that the net serves as a snug decorative covering.

DR. BRUCE KA'IMILOA CHRISMAN

Using a traditional Hawaiian netting pattern, the artist creates a simple sling for a water container.

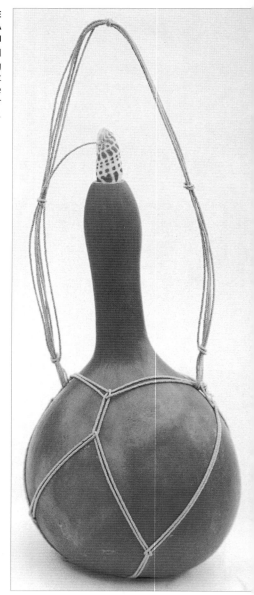

ERIC KELLEY

Designs can be created by leaving some of the spaces open.

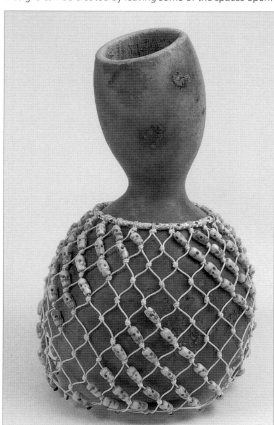

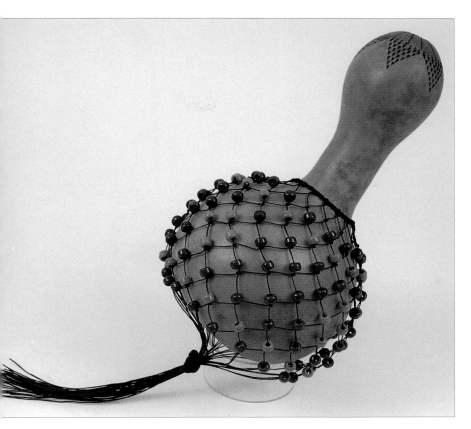

Simple Shekerie

In Africa beads or shells were added to netting to create a popular musical rattle instrument called a shekerie. The shekerie is still a popular instrument in many countries around the world. When the gourd is shaken or slapped, the beads strike the gourd shell and make a pleasing, rhythmic sound. Here's a simple shekerie you can make yourself.

WHAT YOU NEED

Gourd with a large base and a distinct neck (such as a short-handled dipper gourd) or a bottle gourd with a waist and a small bulb at the stem end, cured and cleaned
Electric drill with 1-1/2-inch (3.8 cm) bit
Power or hand cutting tool
Wood-burning tool (optional)
Neutral-colored shoe polish
75 feet (23 m) of waxed linen (or #15 seine cord)
Scissors
Leather awl
100 beads (glass, plastic, or wood), shells or seed pods

WHAT YOU DO

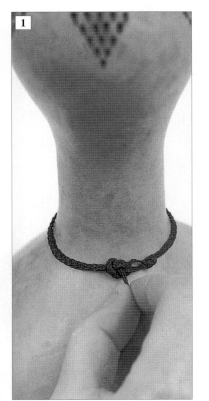

1. Drill a hole at least 1-1/2 (3.8 cm) inches wide in the bottom or cut off the top of the gourd so that you can remove the seeds and pulp. Complete any decorations you want on the gourd prior to doing the netting. In this example, the bulb end was embellished with a wood-burning tool and the surface of the gourd was coated with neutral-colored shoe polish.

2. Make a ring by braiding several strands of the netting material (or you can use a thicker cord, such as a leather thong). The ring should fit loosely around the neck of the gourd (see Photo 1).

3. To determine how long each strand of waxed linen should be, use the following method: Measure the distance from the collar to the bottom of the gourd and add 4 to this number. Multiply this distance by 4. The number of ends of cord you will need depends on the size of your gourd, the density of the netting, and the type of design you want to make with the beads; a good estimate is to mount the cords every 1/4 inch (0.6 cm) on the collar. For this gourd, we cut 16 strands, each 48 inches (121.9 cm) long.

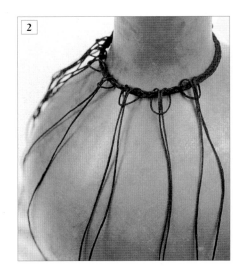

4. Fold each strand in half and mount it to the ring with a lark's head or half-hitch knot, as shown in Photo 2, thus creating two working ends of cord. You can space the cords closely together on the ring or separate them slightly, depending on how dense you want the netting to be.

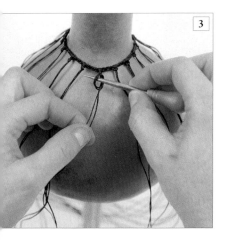

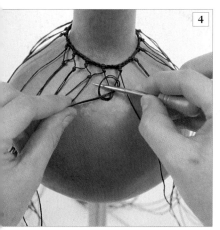

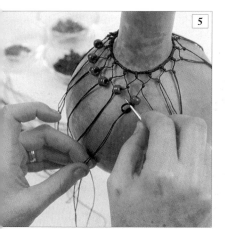

*Thanks to
Rimona Gale
for this project.*

5. Secure each cord in place with an overhand knot that is pulled snug against the lark's head knot (see Photo 3). You can position the overhand knot by placing a leather awl in the knot, where you want it located, before it is cinched tight.

6. Approximately 1/2 inch (1.3 cm) from the first knot, take one strand from each of two adjacent pairs of cords and tie them together with an overhand knot. Again, place the knot precisely with the leather awl (see Photo 4). Continue knotting in this fashion around the gourd.

7. Beginning with the next row of netting, add a bead onto one of the pairs of cord before you tie the knot (see Photo 5). Be sure that you always add the bead to the same side of the pair of cords you are knotting.

8. When all of the rows of netting are complete, gather all the netting cords in your hand (see Photo 6). Hold the shekerie upside down between your knees and twist the cords firmly to make sure you have an even tension on all of the cords. Tie them together in a big overhand knot. Don't tie the knot too close to the bottom, since it is important that the netting fits loosely around the gourd. Leave the ends relatively long; they are often used to pull the netting against the gourd shell during playing.

Knotless netting was worked around the body of this gourd scarecrow from Lombok, Indonesia.

ETHNIC ARTS, BERKELEY, CALIFORNIA

Knotless Netting

There are many patterns that can be created with knotless netting. Historically, it was used by sailors and fishermen to secure floats to nets or to protect their belongings in bouncing boats. (Look for books with old nautical or fancy knot work for more ideas and instruction.)

Knotless netting is the technique used to create the familiar "dream catchers." By working this simple netting in a circle, particularly to fill in an open space, a very interesting spiral web pattern is created, such as was achieved in the photo top left.

To start the knotless netting, you will need to drill holes through the gourd where you will stitch the cord to which the first row of netting will be anchored. After sewing on this line, you can begin to make loops. If the netting is to cover the gourd completely, no other anchor is necessary since the ends will be tied together at the bottom of the gourd. If the knotless netting is going to cover the gourd only partially, you will need to drill holes around the area where you will have your other anchor cord.

Detailed instructions for knotless netting appear in many basketry and handweaving books.

GAIL AND TIM YOUNGBLUTH
Dreamcather Gourd

JANE LUNOW   *Ivy Com'in Round the Mountain*   PHOTO BY JANE ROTHROCK

DIANE ARMSTRONG   *Seashore Bounty*

Teneriffe

Teneriffe is associated with pine needle and raffia baskets as well as with palm leaf baskets from the Marshall Islands. Teneriffe patterns can be created in any opening or against any surface as long as a warp of spokes can be made that radiates from a center. The spokes are then divided into groups and woven separately to create interesting designs.

When working with a gourd, the pattern can be woven around an opening, such as a hole cut in the side of the gourd, around the perimeter of the neck opening, or simply around a circle or other natural shape that is drawn onto the side of a gourd. Natural or dyed raffia is an effective material for weaving teneriffe designs. Most pine needle basketry books contain detailed instructions on how to create teneriffe designs.

DIANE ARMSTRONG   PHOTO BY ROLF MENDEZ

JUDY HICKS   PHOTO BY ROLF MENDEZ

GINGER SUMMIT
This gourd is actually a sampler, with each snowflake on the sides and back showing a different teneriffe pattern.

Tapestry Weaving

Many interesting tapestry effects can be created on a gourd. The basic technique involves threading a foundation warp onto the gourd surface and interweaving it with other yarns or materials. You can achieve a wide range of decorations by varying the design, the area covered by the warp, and the materials used for weaving. It's important to do any staining, coloring, or polishing of the gourd shell before you begin weaving.

KAREN SAVISKAS

REBECCA MARGENAU   *Arizona Snowball*

GINGER SUMMIT

Lacing

Originally, lacing was a method used to repair broken or cracked gourds. The stitching usually was functional and simple. But lacing can also be used as a decorative element, either to join gourd pieces that intentionally have been cut apart or to create a design on a gourd surface. Lacing is also a very effective way to cover or reinforce the top edge of a gourd.

Lacing can be done with any type of material—thread, wire, cord, leather thong, or natural fiber. Simply drill holes along the sides of the crack just large enough for the material (and needle, if one is necessary). If the interior or exterior of the gourd shell has been dyed or painted, it's a good idea to paint the holes before the lacing is done; otherwise the light color of the gourd shell may draw attention to the holes.

DOROTHY MCGUINNESS

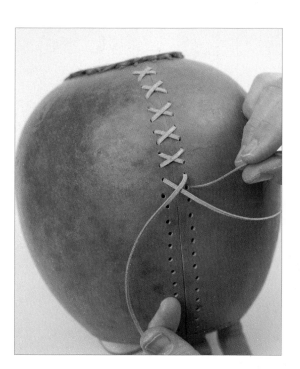

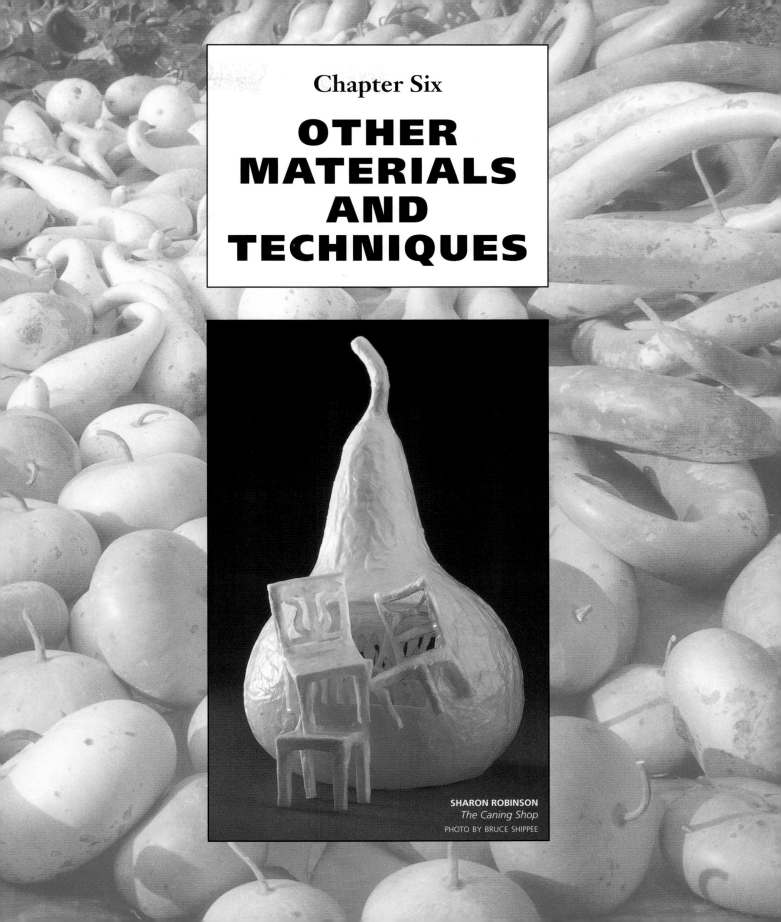

Chapter Six

OTHER MATERIALS AND TECHNIQUES

SHARON ROBINSON
The Caning Shop
PHOTO BY BRUCE SHIPPEE

Clay

Clay can be used in many different ways to build up, cover, or otherwise extend the natural shape of a gourd. Many new kinds of clay are available in hobby and craft-supply stores today, but not all of them are suitable for adding to gourds. For instance, some clays need to be set with heat, and when the gourd is heated along with the clay its shell may become brittle and susceptible to cracking. Also, many kinds of clay shrink while drying and may crack or pull away from the gourd shell. Therefore, look for clay that will harden slowly at room temperatures.

Some clays come in a dry form and need to be mixed with water. These can be used to line the interior of a gourd bowl or tray or to create texture on the outer shell. Before using clay on a gourd, roughen the external shell with sandpaper or a file to create a good bonding surface. If you plan to add clay to the interior, sand the inner shell thoroughly to remove any bits of pulp or the soft spongy layer that may crumble and cause the clay to flake off when it's dry.

You may want to build up a skeleton of metal wire or pegs to serve as a foundation for the clay addition. Firmly anchor the ends of the wire or dowels into the gourd shell so that the appendage is solid. Clay pieces or wedges can be attached to the bottom of a gourd to stabilize it or to provide extra weight to the base. A screw, peg, or nail driven into the gourd base can be wrapped with clay, thus ensuring that it's firmly anchored to the gourd.

LISA LARRIBA   *Bear*

Clay additions can be integrated with the rest of the gourd shell by painting over the clay and the entire gourd surface with an opaque acrylic paint or one of the texture paints. Before you paint, be sure to sand; most clays can be filed and sanded once they are dry. Take extra care to sand the lines where the clay joins the gourd surface. Then, cover the clay addition and the gourd surface with one or more coats of sealer and/or base; this will insure that the final coat of paint will be even over the entire surface of the project. After the last coat of paint has dried, protect it with one or more coats of varnish or polyurethene finish.

DOROTHY GRAFF
He Who Has Water Rules the World

Mosaic Bowl

Clay also can be used to adhere other materials to the gourd surface. The following project uses clay to create a mosaic effect with pieces of abalone shell.

WHAT YOU NEED

Gourd, cured and cleaned
Power or hand cutting tool
Coarse sandpaper
Air-drying clay
Assorted pieces of abalone shell
Damp sponge
Fine sandpaper
White glue
Paintbrush
Leather dye in complementary color
Floor wax

WHAT YOU DO

1. Cut a hole in the gourd to create a container shape and remove the pulp and seeds. Mark the area to be covered with the clay (see Photo 1).

2. Use coarse sandpaper to roughen the shell of the gourd (see Photo 2).

3. Firmly press a layer of the clay onto the gourd, filling the entire sanded area (see Photo 3).

4. Press the abalone pieces into the clay, making sure that the edges are well secured by the clay (see Photo 4). Try to fit the pieces together in such a way that no piece is actually touching another and that there are no large areas without a piece of shell.

5. Use a damp sponge to wipe away excess clay and to clean the gourd shell (see Photo 5). If any shell piece seems loose, press it into the clay and smooth the clay around the edges to hold it in place.

6. Allow the clay to dry completely, which may take several days. If any of the shell pieces come loose during this period, secure them with white glue. If any part of the clay seems rough, sand it gently when dry.

7. Color the gourd and the clay with the leather dye. When dry, finish the surface with several coats of floor wax.

Other Adhesive Materials

Many different types of materials have been used to create an adhesive layer to secure other objects to the gourd surface, including a variety of clay products, wood dough and wood putty, caulking compounds—even tar. Before using any of these materials, roughen the surface of the gourd shell to allow for good bonding. Then press the embellishments—beads, glass, tiles, shells, etc.— into the adhesive layer. Once the adhesive material is completely dry, you can stain or otherwise finish it to blend with the overall gourd design. It's a good idea to then apply several coats of varnish to provide additional bonding for the inlaid objects.

The Huichol Indians of Mexico used beeswax as a bonding agent to secure tiny seed beads or yarn to the interior of gourds. The beeswax was softened in the sun and layered in the clean gourd shell. Because they believed that the gourd was the resting place for the gods and spirits, the Huichol Indians created beautiful and intricate designs of spiritual or cultural significance. A contemporary artist has achieved a similar look with seeds set in beeswax, (see Nancy Lee Schlender's bowls below).

Beads and brass shapes were pressed into a material similar to caulking compound to embellish this gourd from Ghana.
COLLECTION OF GINGER SUMMIT

Gourd bowl interior decorated by Huichol Indians of Mexico with seed beads pressed into beeswax.

COLLECTION OF
SHER LYNN ELLIOT-WIDESS

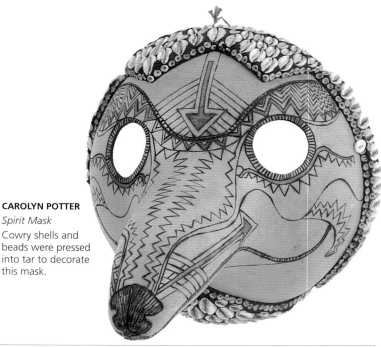

CAROLYN POTTER
Spirit Mask
Cowry shells and beads were pressed into tar to decorate this mask.

NANCY LEE SCHLENDER
Seed Bead Bowl
COLLECTION OF
SHER LYNN ELLIOT-WIDESS

Collage and Decoupage

Decoupage and collage are appealling and simple ways to embellish a gourd. A wide variety of materials can be used, including fabric, netting, yarns and threads; tissue paper, magazine papers, wrapping paper, and handmade paper; natural materials, such as grasses, leaves, sand, and seeds. You can cover the inside and the outside surfaces of the gourd or you can create a collage on just a portion of the gourd.

Before beginning a decoupage or collage project, assemble and shape all of the materials you plan to adhere to the gourd. Select materials that are flexible so that they can conform to the curves of the surface. Cut, tear, or trim papers, fabrics, or other flat materials into workable pieces. Choose an adhesive that is strong enough to secure the materials you have assembled. Several adhesives specifically formulated for paper or fabric collage are available in art and craft-supply stores. For more rigid objects, such as leaves, screen, seeds, or other materials, you may need a stronger adhesive.

If the collage is going to be applied to the interior surface of the gourd, seal it first with varnish or wood sealer and let dry overnight. This will seal the pores of the interior surface, making the gourd suitable for a variety of uses, such as a serving platter or tray.

SANDY WEBSTER *Sarajevo*
A variety of materials were combined in this collage, which were then further embellished with copper wire and multiple shades of dyes.

AVIVA WEINER
This lifelike little lizard is suspended in his own private universe.

SHARON WHEAT
Cheesecloth and other loose fibers were adhered to the gourd shell in a textured collage and then painted and stained to provide a setting for this large bug.

Decoupage Bowl

You can make many attractive variations of this simple gourd bowl.

WHAT YOU NEED

Gourd, cured and cleaned
Power or hand cutting tool
Sandpaper
Leather dye
Paintbrush
Varnish
Collage material
Adhesive

KATHERINE WESTPHAL
Electronic Blossom
Heat transfer color photocopies were adhered to the gourd.

WHAT YOU DO

1. Cut the gourd into a bowl shape and remove the pulp and seeds. Sand all the gourd surfaces.

2. Stain the outside and inside surfaces with leather dye. When dry, varnish all the surfaces. Let dry overnight.

3. Paint both the surface of the gourd and the back of the collage material with the adhesive and press the material to the gourd (see Photo 1). As you add a piece of decorative material, smooth it carefully to remove air bubbles and excess glue. Make sure that the edges are firmly glued down. After each piece is smooth, cover it with another layer of glue (see Photo 2).

4. Continue adding pieces until you complete the design. Then cover the entire interior surface of the gourd and the edges with a coat of adhesive. This secures the edges of the decoupage and gives the gourd an even finish. Some adhesives, when dry, are suitable as a final finish; others should be coated with a varnish or polyurethane. Follow the recommendation of the adhesive manufacturer regarding a final sealant.

JUDY HICKS

Handmade paper is wrapped around this well-dressed gourd.

PHOTO BY ROLF MENDEZ

MAKING PAPER OUT OF GOURD PULP

Usually most people clean out the interior of a gourd and discard all the mess as quickly as possible. You may want to save some of the seeds in hopes that next year you can grow more gourds just like the ones you now have. But there is a good use for the remainder of the pulp: You can make paper! Paper making is easy, fun, and opens up a whole new arena of gourd craft. Many books are available that describe paper making in detail. Here's the recipe to get your handmade gourd paper started.

Gourd pulp by itself doesn't have fibers that are long enough to create a strong paper, so it should be mixed with another pulp, such as cut-up rags or scrap paper. Be sure to remove the seeds from the gourd pulp. Start with approximately one quart of gourd pulp, firmly packed. Boil it for at least three hours, adding two tablespoons of trisodiumphosphate (sold as TSP in most hardware stores) to help break down the gourd fibers. Allow it to cool. Place approximately 1/2 cup each of the gourd pulp and the soaked paper into a blender. Add enough water to fill the blender approximately half full. Blend the mixture for about 15 seconds and stop to check the consistency of the mixture. It can be slightly lumpy, but the smoother the mixture, the more even the paper will be.

Pour the blended pulp into a holding basin and repeat with new pulp until you have several cups of pulp. Fill a plastic dish pan approximately 1/2 full with water, and add several cups of the pulp, swishing it around to make the solution free of lumps. Continue now as you would with any other paper pulp.

Examples of paper made from gourd pulp

Figures

DOLLS

In museums and private collections there are surprisingly few old gourds that were fashioned into children's toys. Some whistles, tops, and balls have been identified, and rare artifacts of gourd dolls indicate that gourds were used in this way, but few have survived. The shapes and contours of gourds themselves suggest that they were used as dolls in the past.

Today, artists and crafts people use gourds to create many different types of dolls. Some have heads made with small dipper gourds, with the handle of the gourd sewn into a body. Others have gourd heads and limbs attached to cloth bodies. And some dolls are constructed entirely of gourds. The simplest type of gourd doll can be created by painting a face and some clothes on an appropriately shaped bottle gourd.

SUSAN SMREKAR

MARY WOJECK
This doll with a gourd face has gourd arms and legs as well.

Sandra Blaylock and Gabriel Cyr
Gourdian Spirit
PHOTO BY BOB BARRETT

ALEX MACDONALD

KACHINAS

Gourds were frequently recognized by prehistoric cultures as having a special relationship to the spirit world. Mythology and folktales from around the globe express the special ways that gourds were regarded as vehicles for communicating with the forces of the invisible world.

In very early cultures humans personified these unknown forces by creating images or by dressing in special costumes to personify individual spirits. Gourds were occasionally used to make fetishes or otherwise represent individual spirits. Contemporary artists carry on this tradition of spirit dolls with new interpretations.

NANCY LEE SCHLENDER
Papoose #2

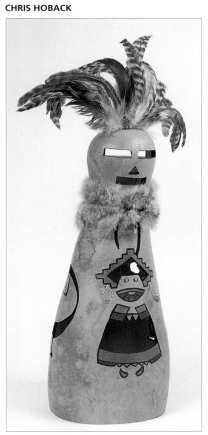

JOLEE SCHLEA
Gourd Maiden with Vessel
PHOTO BY KIRK SCHLEA

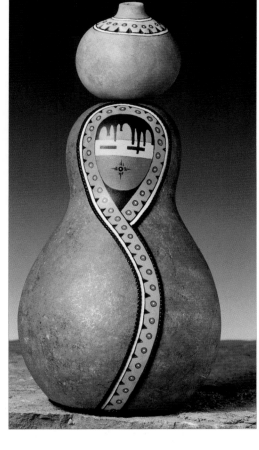

CHRIS HOBACK

NANCY TELLO

PUPPETS

A related use for gourds is for making puppets. By using the gourd as the head, other material can be draped over the puppeteer's arm to form the clothing or body of the puppet. If the puppet is intended for serious play, look for a small hardshell gourd; ornamental gourds, although the right size, often have thin shells and are likely to break. The stem end of the gourd can be used as a nose (or a trunk!) or it can be attached to the puppet body as a neck. The wide variety of shapes and sizes of gourds suggests a fantasy land for storytelling.

SHER LYNN ELLIOTT-WIDESS
Crow Mother

Santa Puppet

This Santa puppet uses the shape of the gourd itself to create an unforgettable yuletide nose.

WHAT YOU NEED

Small hardshell gourd,
  cured and cleaned
Electric drill with 1/4-inch (0.6 cm)
  and 1/16-inch (1.5 mm) bits
Small paintbrush
Acrylic or tempera paints
Scissors
Newspaper
Red fabric, 10 x 15 inches (25 x 38 cm)
Sewing machine and sewing thread
Scraps of black felt
Polyester fleece, 10 inches (25 cm)
White glue
Metal skewer
Unspun fleece
Sharp knife
Keyhole saw
Curved tapestry needle
Heavy-gauge thread

WHAT YOU DO

1. Paint the face, using a mixture of pinks to give Santa a rosy glow. Allow the paint to dry.

2. Make a robe for the puppet in the shape of a cross. Use your own hand and arm to determine measurements that will be comfortable for you. As a general guideline, the distance from the hem to the neck should be about 12 inches (30 cm), allowing about 3 inches (7.5 cm) for the neck to be attached to the puppet head. The distance between the puppet hands should be about 8 inches (20 cm) (see Figure 1). Use newspaper to make a pattern to make sure the dimensions fit both your hand and the puppet head. Then cut two pieces of fabric for the body and sew the shoulder and side seams. Cut out mittens from the black felt; cut off two bands from the fleece.

For the hat, make a newspaper pattern, cutting a semicircle until it fits the dimensions of the gourd head. Cut out the hat from red fabric. Sew the semicircle into a cone (see Figure 2) and then stitch on a band of fleece.

3. Drill 1/4-inch (0.6 cm) holes in all of the areas where the hair and beard will be attached (see Photo 1).

4. Put a dab of glue in one of the holes and use a skewer to push the end of a small amount of fleece into the hole (see Photo 2). Continue to fill all the holes you have drilled with bits of fleece (see Photo 3). When all the hair is in place, let the glue dry completely.

5. Use the keyhole saw to cut a hole on the bottom of Santa's head that is large enough to fit at least two fingers. Clean out all the seeds and pulp. Drill 1/16-inch (1.5 mm) holes around the large hole, spaced about 1 inch (2.5 cm) apart (see Photo 4).

6. Put plenty of glue around the large hole and on the edge of the robe that will be attached to the gourd head to form the puppet's body (see Photo 5).

7. Stitch the robe onto the gourd through the small holes (see Photo 6).

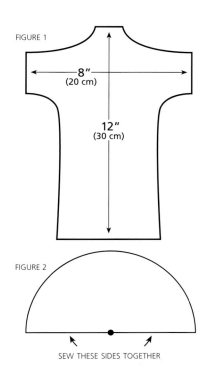

FIGURE 1

8" (20 cm)

12" (30 cm)

FIGURE 2

SEW THESE SIDES TOGETHER

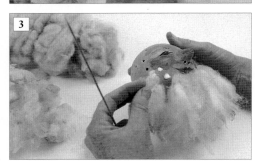

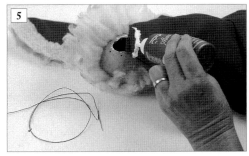

MASKS

Masks constructed of gourds were often used in special ceremonies by primitive cultures worldwide. Gourd masks were usually part of an elaborate costume used to invoke or impersonate the spirits. In Africa the mask became a symbol of control when worn by a powerful member of a tribe, such as the shaman. When fully dressed, the wearer became an apparition of the superhuman force invoked to ward off evil or to reinforce law and order. Masks were also important in North American Indian ceremonies, particularly in the Southwest pueblo tribes, as parts of costumes that all members of a group or secret society wore as they danced in tribal ceremonies. Gourds were used as the foundation of the mask face or as an element such as a beak, mouth, nose, ears, or horns.

Masks are rarely worn today, except by children and for special holidays such as Halloween and Mardi Gras. However, they are often made by artists for display. Every decorative technique discussed in the book can be used to create gourd masks: They can be carved, wood burned, joined, painted, and embellished with any type of material. The only requirement for making a gourd mask is a lively imagination!

BETZ SALMONT
PHOTO BY ARTIST

KATHLEEN KREBS

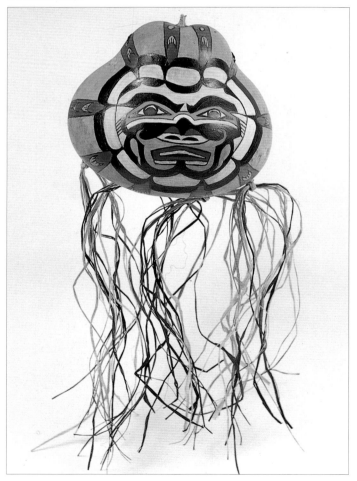

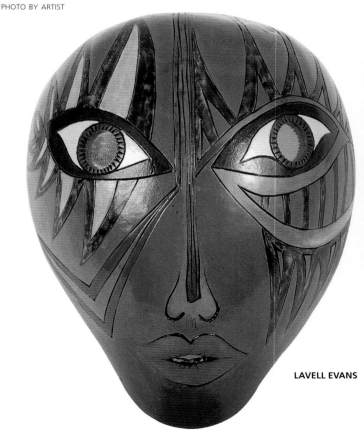

LAVELL EVANS

MARY WOJECK
This mask was clearly designed and made to be worn.
PHOTO BY EVAN BRACKEN

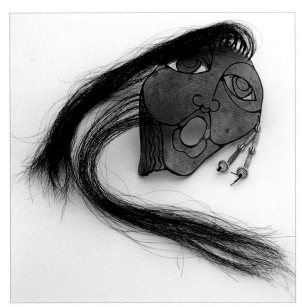

BEVERLY SHAMANA

KAY HATTEN

**JERRALDINE
MASTEN
HANSEN**

PHOTO BY
GREGG WURTZ

Other Applications

HOLIDAY DECORATIONS

A bowl of brightly colored ornamental gourds is a familiar sight during autumn, and as the project on page 90 demonstrates, dried and painted ornamentals make wonderful Halloween decorations. The variety of gourd shapes available is sure to suggest witches, ghosts, and other mysterious goblins. Try carving a large gourd instead of a pumpkin; to avoid a potential fire hazard, be sure to encase a candle inside a glass container.

However, embellished gourds make terrific holiday decorations throughout the year, as the examples on the next few pages beautifully demonstrate. As tree ornaments, supplements on a wreath, or a jolly Santa on the window seat, gourds can be right at home during Christmas.

Small ornamental gourds can be used to decorate a table or bowl in other seasons as well. In spring lovely flowers made from cut ornamentals can blossom on a dried branch (see the project on page 32). Small gourd birds can perch in dried arrangements, on branches, or in nests by themselves. Gourd Easter eggs can brighten an Easter basket constructed from a bushel gourd. In the summer try floating ornamental gourd fish in a small bowl.

Most frequently ornamental gourds are painted with acrylic, temperas, or watercolors. To ensure that they will last for many seasons, it's important to give them several coats of varnish. If the gourd has been properly dried and cleaned, it should be useful for many years.

GINGER SUMMIT
Christmas Ornaments

STONY RIDGE
Easter Basket

GINGER SUMMIT
Halloween Ornaments

SUSAN FORREST

KERRY AND JAMIE DEVRIENT, Terra Nova Gourdworks
Spring Rabbit with Violets

JEWELRY

Gourd scraps can be transformed into attractive and light-weight earrings, pins, and barrettes. Pencil in the shape of your jewelry on a gourd scrap and cut out the piece with a motorized cutting tool. Sand the backs of the pieces. If you are making a barrette, you will need to make a groove with the cutting tool for gluing on a metal-clip backing (wood glue is a good choice). You can paint, stain, carve, or wood burn a design. Allow the jewelry to dry and then spray it with polyurethane.

NANCY LEE SCHLENDER
*Gourd seed necklace
with pendant*

JOHN MCGUIRE
PHOTO BY ARTIST

SCOTT JOHNSON
Pendant necklace

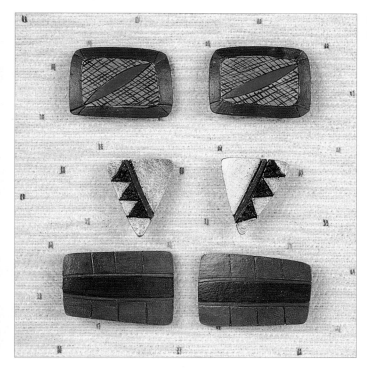

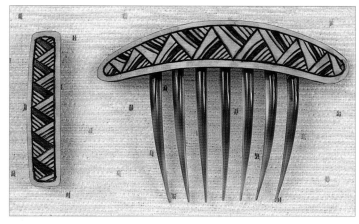

MUSICAL INSTRUMENTS

One of the first applications that man made of gourds was as musical instruments. Indeed, there is speculation that the very first instrument, aside from a stick, was the gourd. Gourd instruments were used by every ancient culture in temperate zones around the world, and they continue to be used today for that purpose in many parts of the world (see page 8 for more examples).

The very earliest gourd instruments were probably simple shakers or rattles. With no modification the gourd provided soft rhythmic accompaniment to movement or chanting, and with only the slight addition of stones or seeds the level of sound was greatly increased. By slapping the gourd it became a drum, later to be modified by the addition of a membrane or head. By cutting blow holes in the top or sides the gourds became whistles or horns.

More sophisticated developments entailed using the gourd as a resonating box to amplify the sounds of strings, plucked tongs, or sounding boards hit with mallets. The tremendous versatility of gourds combined with the creative ingenuity of men through the ages is reflected in a wonderful variety of instruments that continue to entertain and delight both performers and audiences today.

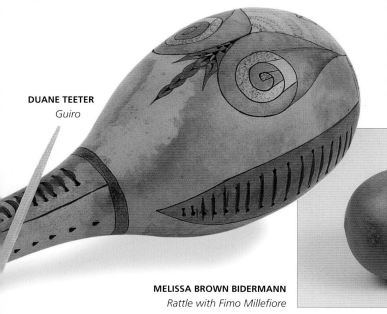

DUANE TEETER
Guiro

MELISSA BROWN BIDERMANN
Rattle with Fimo Millefiore

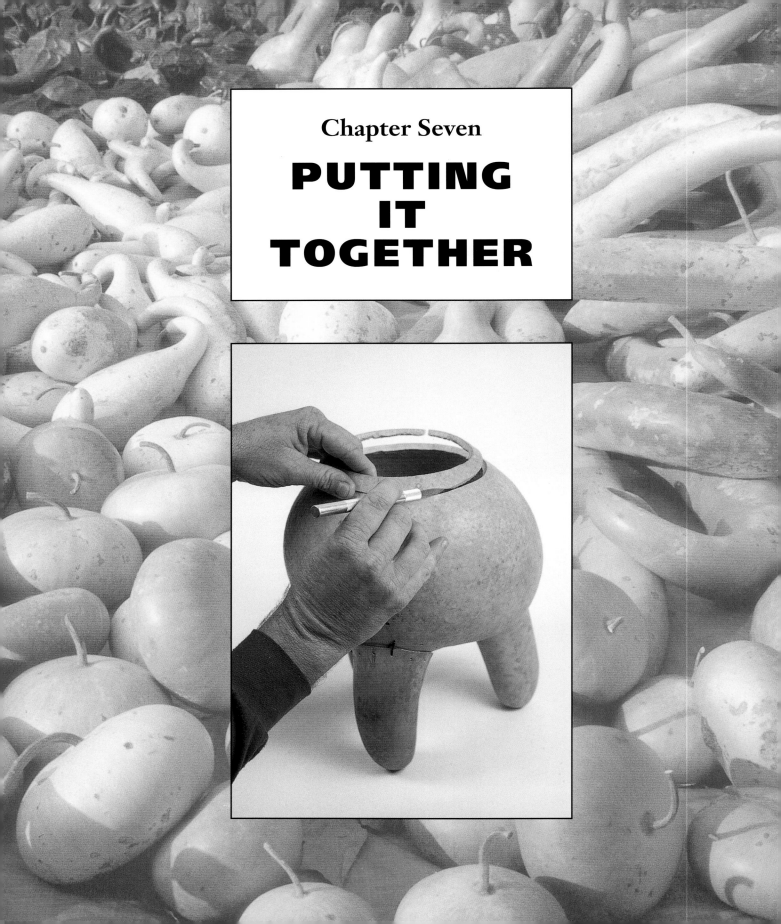

Chapter Seven
PUTTING IT TOGETHER

A Project in Pictures

DON WEEKE, *an artist living in southern California, has been embellishing gourds with basketry techniques for many years. His distinctive style combines these techniques with many other decorative methods, including pyrography, carving, and painting. His gourd art can be seen in galleries and private collections around the United States.*

Don also is a popular teacher of gourd craft. We asked him to design a project that would incorporate attaching gourd pieces to a main gourd body, wood-burning, carving, painting, and basketry. The aim was to illustrate how these basic techniques can be brought together to create a striking gourd sculpture.

MATERIALS

4 bottle gourds, 1 larger than the rest
Handsaw or power saw
Pencil
Electric drill with 1/8-inch (0.3 cm) bit
Black waxed linen thread
Wood burner with broad and fine tips
Brown leather dye
Fine-tip paintbrush
Black enamel paint
Date palm
Scissors
Needle-nose pliers
Power carving tool

Don used a large bottle gourd for the container. His first step was to cut three legs from the necks of other bottle gourds, shaping them to fit the contour of the curved bottom of the large gourd container (not shown). The piece was finished by coiling date palm around the neck of the container to mirror the curvature of the gourd body. The other main steps are shown on the following pages.

1.

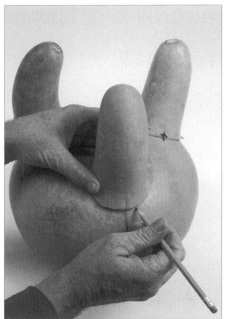

Tracing around a leg on the bottom of the container

2.

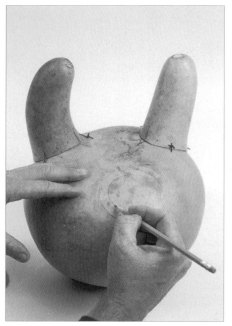

Drawing a smaller circle inside the traced outline to allow the leg to be braced snugly against the surface of the larger gourd

3.

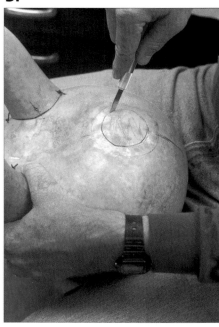

Cutting around the inside circle with a small handsaw

4.

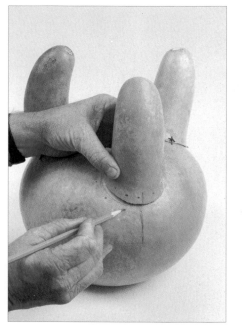

Repositioning the leg to mark with a pencil exactly where four holes should be drilled on both the container and the leg

5.

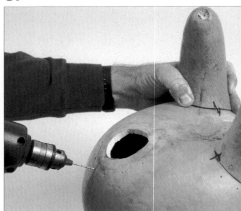

Drilling holes in the container

6.

Drilling holes in the leg

7.

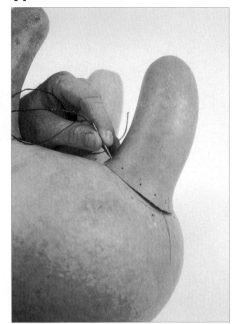

Threading the waxed linen through the holes in the leg and then in the gourd body

8.

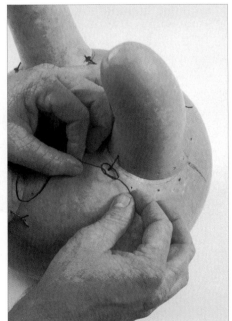

Tying the thread to hold the leg securely in place (repeated for all three legs)

9.

Marking a level line around the opening of the gourd

10.

Cutting along the line with a small handsaw

11.

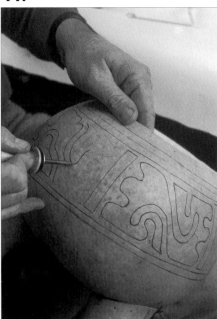

Wood burning the pencilled outline of a design on the body of the gourd

12.

Staining the entire gourd surface, including the legs, with leather dye

13.

Painting a broad stripe of black enamel around the gourd body

14.

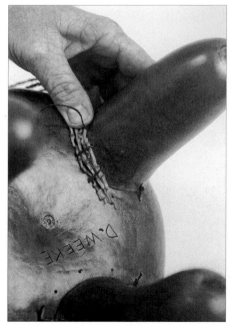

Couching several strands of date palm around the base of the legs to hide the join

15.

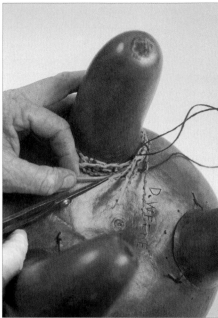

Tapering the ends of the date palm to keep the thickness of the couching uniform around the leg

16.

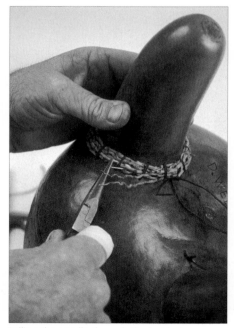

Pulling the needle through the last hole

17.

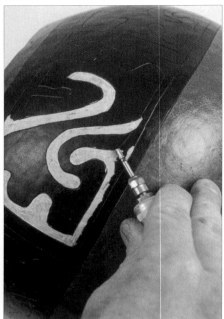

Using a power tool to carve away the background of the design that was wood-burned on the gourd body

18.

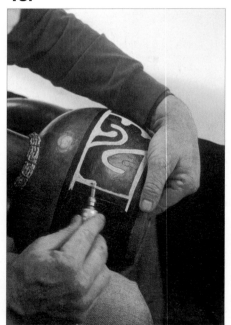

Creating a dramatic black silhouette

Acknowledgements

This book is the result of the sharing of time, energy, and ideas of many people united by their special enthusiasm for the gourd. So many people contributed in so many different ways that it's difficult to single out individuals. This book was made possible by the support and lively interest of the entire gourd community.

First of all we want to thank our families—Roger Summit and Sher and Andy Widess—for putting up with chaotic schedules and cluttered spaces for such a long time. The staff at The Caning Shop—Shelly Moore, Peeta Tinay, and Roberto Lazo—also provided wonderful support, allowing us, not only the time, but the space to work, write, collect art work, and communicate with contributors. Thanks also to Jenny Brunswig for providing studio space for all the craft work and photography.

Special thanks also to Rimona Gale and Don Weeke for allowing us to photograph them while creating their work for chapters five and seven.

All of the research and information gathering was made possible by Dialog Information Services, Inc. This body of information confirmed to us not only that a new book was appropriate now, but also led us to individuals, crafts people, and collections we would never have discovered otherwise.

Although many museums have wonderful gourd collections, we extend a special appreciation to the staffs at the New York Museum of Natural History in New York City, New York, the Maxwell Museum in Albuquerque, New Mexico, The Kauai Museum in Kauai, Hawaii, the Museum of Appalachia in Norris, Tennessee, and Larry Dawson at the Phoebe Hearst Museum in Berkeley, California. We also were honored to view the private collections of Len and Anna Shemin (Nomadic Traders) in Berkeley, California, The Marvin Johnson Museum in Fuquay Varina, North Carolina, and Minnie Black in East Bernstadt, Kentucky.

Gourd growers Jim Story, Kern Ackerman, Glen Burkhalter, and Suzanne Ashworth generously shared their expertise in growing and identifying these wonderfully varied plants.

This book is enriched by the contributions and suggestions of many outstanding artists. The names of those whose gourds appears in the book are listed on pages 140–141. Dozens of other talented artists sent us examples of their gourd art but, unfortunately, we were not able to include them all. We feel privileged to have been able to enjoy such a high level of creativity and generosity.

A special thank you goes to editor Deborah Morgenthal, who tirelessly guided us through the process of turning our ambitious dreams into a lovely reality.

The American Gourd Society

The purpose of the American Gourd Society is:

To promote horticultural and ethnological research in gourds; to publish books, pamphlets, bulletins; to encourage the use of gourds in decorative art; to hold exhibits.

The AGS has its roots in organizations that were first started in 1934 in California, and in 1937 in Massachusetts. Currently, it is based in Mt. Gilead, Ohio, and boasts a membership of more than 5,000, with representation from all states and many foreign countries.

While based in New England, AGS sponsored and published several scholarly monographs on gourd history and culture that continue to be a valuable source of information and education today. In addition, AGS has published several other booklets and bulletins that describe horticulture and simple craft projects. AGS also publishes the quarterly *Gourd* newsletter, which includes a list of growers who sell seeds and gourds of all types.

Several of the gourd society chapters sponsor annual gourd shows. The World's Largest Gourd Show, sponsored by the Ohio chapter, is held annually the first weekend in October in Mt. Gilead, Ohio. It attracts participants from around the country as well as international visitors. Displays and competitions are held in 85 categories, including green and dried gourds and every imaginable craft and art application. Speakers, demonstrations, and entertainment all contribute to a memorable gourd extravaganza. The Australian chapter hosts an annual gourd show called "Gourds and Gammas" (the Australian term for squash).

Contributing Artists

Deb Abrahamson, page 100
Seattle, Washington

Joseph Adotta, page 91
Santa Monica, California

Linda Arias, page 74
Los Angeles, California

Diane Armstrong, pages 49, 113, and 114
Wrightwood, California

Pam Barton, pages 36 and 96
Volcano, Hawaii

Peggy Baumgartner, page 60
Vinemont, Alabama

Cheryln Bennett, page 78
Reno, Nevada

Melissa Brown Bidermann, page 133
Granada Hills, California

Minnie Black, page 47
East Bernstadt, Kentucky

Sandra Blaylock, 124
Asheville, North Carolina

Janice Bolander, page 74
Kingston, Illinois

Susan Van Dyke Bridges, page 96
Charlotte, North Carolina

Selma Brown, page 42
San Francisco, California

Steve and Sue Buck, page 93
Stockton, California

Glenn Burkhalter, page 20
Lacy Spring, Alabama

Susan Cantwell-Hernandez, page 73
Rancho Palos Verdes, California

Gretchen Ceteras, page 40
Rumsey, California

Bruce Ka'imiloa Chrisman,
pages 58 and 110
Honokaa, Hawaii

Gaye Cook, page 26
Sonoma, California

Susan Correia, page 39
Castro Valley, California

Liz Cunningham, pages 35 and 92
Freestone, California

Gabriel Cyr, page 124
Asheville, North Carolina

Kerry and Jamie Devrient, pages 83 and 131
Jackson, Mississippi

Ami Diallo, pages 13, 51, and 52
Embudo, New Mexico

Linda Egleston, page 64
Patagonia, Arizona

Ruth Ehrenkrantz, pages 70 and 78
Berkeley, California

Sher Lynn Elliott-Widess, page 126
Berkeley, California

Lavell Evans, pages 66 and 128
Bisbee, Arizona

Carola Farthing, page 104
Mill Valley, California

Susan Forrest, page 131
Sturgeon, Missouri

Rimona Gale, pages 30 and 111
El Sobrante, California

M.C. Glenn, pages 42 and 53
Pangburn, Arkansas

Maurice Gosden, page 26
Bendigo, Australia

Dorothy Graff, pages 118 and 133
Chico, California

Eugenia Gwathney, pages 39 and 50
Sacramento, California

Henrietta Haines, page 48
Los Angeles, California

Hal Hall, page 81
Kent, Ohio

Jerraldine Masten Hansen,
pages 74, 101, and 129
Monterey, California

Kay Hatten, page 129
Fremont, California

R.K. Hejny, pages 71 and 99
Houston, Texas

Orlando Hernandez, page 110
San Francisco, California

Mary Hettmansperger, page 101
Peru, Indiana

Judy Hicks, pages 114 and 123
Wrightwood, California

Chris Hoback,
pages 26, 51, 70, 100, and 125
San Ramon, California

John Horne, page 89
Hyattsville, Missouri

Marilyn Host, pages 43, 61, and 96
San Martin, California

Robin Ann Hunter, page 33
Albuquerque, New Mexico

Carol Ann Johnson, page 23
Hillsboro, Oregon

Scott Johnson, page 132
Chico, California

Eric Kelley, page 110
Portland, Oregon

Kathleen Krebs, page 128
Berkeley, California

Ridge Kunzel, pages 73 and 82
Sequim, Washington

Bill Kupka, pages 47 and 96
Chelsea, Iowa

Lisa Larriba, pages 68, 93, and 118
Santa Barbara, California

Dick Lewis, pages 47 and 52
Preble, New York

Jennifer Loe, page 80
Berkeley, California

Elizabeth Loftus, page 87
Marshfield, Massachusetts

Elaine Long, page 68
Manistee, Michigan

Jane Lunow, page 113
Hickory, North Carolina

Rebecca Margenau, page 115
Eldersburg, Maryland

Karen Martin, page 64
Cincinatti, Ohio

Deborah Martinez-Rambeau, page 92
Los Angeles, California

Alex MacDonald, pages 50, 75, and 124
Julian, California

Susan McGann, page 33
Seattle, Washington

Dorothy McGuinness, page 116
Seattle, Washington

John McGuire, pages 106 and 132
Geneva, New York

Leslie Miller, pages 88 and 91
Deceased

Lupe Molina, page 82
Joshua Tree, California

Carol Morrison, page 133
Palo Alto, California

Deborah Moskowitz, pages 42 and 106
Sedro-Woolley, Washington

Deborah Muhl, page 100
Spinnerstown, Pennsylvania

Judy Mulford, pages 81 and 104
Los Angeles, California

Debbie Norton, page 78
Lake Almanor, California

Suzye Ogawa, page 91
Santa Monica, California

Lorraine Oller, page 71
Berkeley, California

Ethel Owen, page 49
Birmingham, Alabama

Bob Patterson, page 110
Orinda, California

Eva Pawlak, page 32
Highland Heights, Ohio

Dyan Peterson, page 50
Swannanoa, North Carolina

Rowena Philbeck, page 68
Hearne, Texas

Larry Phillips, page 43
San Juan Pueblo, New Mexico

Carolyn Potter, page 120
Pasadena, California

Mary Pryor, page 55
Anaheim, California

Marilyn Rehm, page 96
Big Prairie, Ohio

Beverly Robbins, page 41
Weed, California

Sharon Robinson, page 118
Santa Rosa, California

Jeanette Roll, page 64
Fallbrook, California

Carolyn Rushton, page 83
Glenwood, Indiana

Betz Salmont, page 128
Manhattan Beach, California

Sheila Satow, page 93
Los Angeles, California

Karen Saviskas, page 115
West Hills, California

Jolee Schlea, pages 15, 56, and 125
San Diego, California

Nancy Lee Schlender,
page 63, 99, 120, 125, and 132
Houston, Texas

Janeice Scofield, page 64
Eugene, Oregon

Beverly Shamana, pages 104 and 129
Los Angeles, California

Roy Schick, pages 73 and 82
Sequim, Washington

Susan Smrekar, page 124
Millston, Wisconsin

Donna Soszynski, pages 61 and 70
Corte Madera, California

Jean Stone, page 34
Burwood, Australia

Stony Ridge, page 130
Magalia, Washington

Jim Story, page 21
Pendleton, Indiana

Ginger Summit, pages 54, 59, 87, 92, 95,
99, 100, 109, 114, 115, 130, and 131
Los Altos Hills, California

Susan Sweet, pages 43 and 66
Booneville, California

Duane Teeter, page 53, 55, and 133
Sacramento, California

Nancy Tello, pages 79 and 125
Guerneville, California

Kris Thoeni, pages 60 and 101
Santa Cruz, California

Nan Toothman, pages 50 and 83
Moorehead City, North Carolina

Mayumi Tsukuda, page 51
Kiyomi Ono-gun Gifu, Japan

Mimi Turner, page 42
Marshfield, Massachusetts

Joseph Ulmer, page 34
Sebastopol, California

Gayna Uransky, page 101
Garberville, California

Eva Walsh, pages 106 and 109
Winterpark, Florida

Sandy Webster, page 73 and 121
Brasstown, North Carolina

Don Weeke, page 97 and 135 to 138
Ramona, California

Aviva Weiner, page 121
Los Angeles, California

Diane Westgate, page 40
Sonora, California

Katherine Westphal, page 122
Berkeley, California

Sharon Wheat, page 121
Berkeley, California

Denise Windwalker, page 106
Stagecoach, Nevada

Mary Wojeck, pages 46, 124, and 129
Travelers Rest, South Carolina

Gail and Tim Youngbluth, pages 93 and 113
Barksdale Airforce Base, Louisiana

S.D. Youngwolf, pages 74 and 133
Kingston, Arizona

Lorraine Zielinski, pages 86 and 88
Manistee, Michigan

From the Collections of Artists, Museums, and Galleries

Peggy Baumgartner, page 37
Vinemont, Alabama

Peter Bohley, pages 8 and 9
Saratoga, California

Casa Antigua, pages 48 and 98
Redwood City, California

Ami Diallo, page 6
Embudo, New Mexico

Ethnic Arts, pages 76 and 112
Berkeley, California

Sher Lynn Elliott-Widess, page 120
Berkeley, California

Norma Fox, page 57
Berkeley, California

Eugenia, Gwathney, pages 10 and 98
Sacramento, California

Chris Hoback, pages 57 and 86
San Ramon, California

Kauai Museum, page 58
Kauai, Hawaii

David King, page 84
Richmond, California

Kathie McDonald, pages 54 and 77
Concord, California

Carol Morrison, page 98
Palo Alto, California

Judy Mulford, page 7
Los Angeles, California

Phoebe Hearst Museum, pages 6 and 7
Berkeley, California

Len and Anna Shemin,
pages 58, 76, 77, and 85
Berkeley, California

Jean Struthers, page 11
Los Altos Hills, California

Ginger Summit, pages 9, 10, 11, 84, and 120
Los Altos Hills, California

Dick and Beanie Wezelman,
pages 10 and 85
Berkeley, California

Andy Widess, page 9
Berkeley, California

Jim Widess, page 84
Berkeley, California

Supply Sources

Gourd Seeds

SUZANNE ASHWORTH
5007 Del Rio Road
Sacramento, CA 95822-2514

AMERICAN GOURD SOCIETY
Box 274
Mt. Gilead, OH 43338-0274

ROCKY FORD GOURDS
c/o Kern Ackerman
178 Losee Street, Box 222
Cygnet, OH 43413

NICHOLS GARDEN NURSERY
1190 North Pacific Hwy.
Albany, OR 97321-4598

Luffas

RUSS GUIRL
Route 2, Box 535-B
Sheridan, AK 72150

TERRY HOLDSCLAW
Box 85
Terrell, NC 28682

Gourds

THE GOURD FACTORY
P.O. Box 9
Linden, CA 95236

THE GOURD FARM
c/o Lena Braswell
Route 1, Box 73
Wrens, GA 30833

THE PUMPKIN AND GOURD FARM
101 Creston Road
Paso Robles, CA 93446

DOUG AND SUE WELBURN
Route 6, Box 77
Fallbrook, CA 92028

WEST MOUNTAIN GOURD FARM
Route 1, Box 853
Gilmer, TX 75644

OZARK COUNTRY CREATIONS
Dennis and Becky Hatfield
30226 Holly Road
Pierce City, MO 65723

JOHN VAN TOL
P.O. Box 298
East Maitland
NSW 2323 Australia

Dyes

FIEBING'S LEATHER DYES
516 S. 2nd Street
Milwaukee, WI 53204

LINCOLN LEATHER DYES
172 Commercial Street
Sunnyvale, CA 94086

TANDY LEATHER SUPPLY
P.O. Box 791
Fort Worth, TX 76101
(Can tell you local distributor)

THE LEATHER FACTORY
Advertising Department
3847 East Loop, 820 South
Fort Worth, TX 76105
(Can tell you local distributor)

Basketry Materials

H.H. PERKINS
10 South Bradley Road
Woodbridge, CT 06525

ROYALWOOD LTD.
517 Woodville Road
Mainsfield, OH 44907

THE CANING SHOP
926 Gilman Street
Berkeley, CA 94710
800-544-3373

Wood-Burning and Carving Tools

THE WOODWORKERS' STORE
4365 Willow Drive
Medina, MN 55340

CRAFT WOODS
2101 Green Spring Drive
Timonium, MD 21093

WOODCRAFT
210 Wood County Industrial Park
Box 1686
Parkersburg, WV 26102-1686

THE CANING SHOP
926 Gilman Street
Berkeley, CA 94710
800-544-3373

Bibliography

Bailey, L. H. *The Garden of Gourds.* Mt. Gilead, Ohio: Barber Press, Inc., 1956 (reprinted 1980).

Beckwith, Carol and Marion Van Offelen. *Nomads of Niger.* New York: Harry N. Abrams, 1983.

Berns, Marla and Barbara Rubin Hudson. *The Essential Gourd.* Los Angeles, California: Museum of Cultural History, University of California, 1986.

Boyer, Robert. *The Amazing Art of Pyrography.* Evanston, Illinois: Evanston Publishing Inc., 1992.

Carlson, Eric, Dawn Cusick, and Carol Taylor. *The Complete Book of Nature Crafts.* Emmaus, Pennsylvania: Rodale Press, 1992.

Dagan, Esther. *When Art Shares Nature's Gifts.* Montreal, P.Q., H3G 1L3 Canada: Galerie Amrad African Arts, 1988.

Dodge, Ernest S. *Hawaiian and Other Polynesian Gourds.* Honolulu, Hawaii: Topgallant Publishing Co., Ltd., 1978.

Gottsegen, Mark D. *The Painter's Handbook.* New York: Watson Guptill Publications, 1993.

Gourd Society of America. *Gourds, Their Culture and Art.* Mt. Gilead, Ohio: American Gourd Society, Inc., 1966.

Grant, Bruce. *Leather Braiding.* Centreville, Maryland: Cornell Maritime Press, Inc., 1950.

Menzie, Eleanor. *Hand Carved and Decorated Gourds of Peru.* Santa Monica, California: Karneke Publishing, 1976.

Heiser, Charles B., Jr. *The Gourd Book.* Norman, Oklahoma: University of Oklahoma Press, 1979.

—— *Of Plants and People.* Norman, Oklahoma: University of Oklahoma Press, 1985.

Mayer, Ralph. *The Artist's Handbook of Materials and Techniques.* New York: Viking Press, Penguin Books, 1991.

Graburn, Nelson. *Ethnic and Tourist Arts; Cultural Expressions from Around the World.* Berkeley, California: University of California Press, 1979.

Milanich, Jerald T. *Archaeology of Pre-columbian Florida.* Gainesville, Florida: University Press of Florida, 1994.

Nabhan, Gary Paul. *Gathering the Desert.* Tucson, Arizona: University of Arizona Press, 1985.

Newman, Thelma R. *Contemporary African Arts and Crafts.* New York: Crown Publishers, Inc., 1974.

Prawat Mordecai, Carolyn. *Gourd Craft.* Mt. Gilead, Ohio: American Gourd Society, Inc., 1978.

Price, Sally and Richard. *Afro-American Arts of the Suriname Rain Forest.* Los Angeles, California: Museum of Cultural History, University of California, 1980.

Richardson, Helen, ed. *Fibre Basketry Homegrown and Handmade.* The Fibre Basket Weavers of South Australia, Inc. Kenthurst, NSW: Kangaroo Press, 1989.

Speck, Frank G. *Gourds of the Southeastern Indians.* Mt. Gilead, Ohio: Hartman Printing Co., Inc., 1941.

Stearns, Lynn. *Papermaking for Basketry and Other Crafts.* Asheville, North Carolina: Lark Books, 1992.

Stribling, Mary Lou. *North American Indian Arts.* New York: Crown Publishers, Inc., 1975.

Wilson, Eddie W. *The Gourd in Folk Literature.* Mt. Gilead, Ohio: Gourd Society of America, Hartman Printing Co., 1947.

Wojeck, Mary. *Crafts From the Gourd Patch.* Mary Wojeck, 175 Mark Beech Rd., Marietta, South Carolina 29661, 1987.

Wolf, Joan. *A Guide to Burning Techniques.* Colwood Electronics, 1 Meridian Rd., Eatontown, NJ 07720, 1989.

Index